Political Argument in a Polarized Age

Political Argument in a Polarized Age

Reason and Democratic Life

Scott F. Aikin and Robert B. Talisse

polity

First published in 2020 by Polity Press

Polity Press
65 Bridge Street
Cambridge CB2 1UR, UK

Polity Press
101 Station Landing
Suite 300
Medford, MA 02155, USA

ISBN-13: 978-1-5095-3652-8
ISBN-13: 978-1-5095-3653-5(pb)

A catalogue record for this book is available from the British Library.

Typeset in 10 on 16.5pt Charter
by Fakenham Prepress Solutions, Fakenham, Norfolk NR21 8NL
Printed and bound in the UK by CPI Group (UK) Ltd, Croydon

The publisher has used its best endeavours to ensure that the URLs for external websites referred to in this book are correct and active at the time of going to press. However, the publisher has no responsibility for the websites and can make no guarantee that a site will remain live or that the content is or will remain appropriate.

Every effort has been made to trace all copyright holders, but if any have been overlooked the publisher will be pleased to include any necessary credits in any subsequent reprint or edition.

For further information on Polity, visit our website: politybooks.com

Contents

Acknowledgments

We are two remarkably fortunate authors. For one thing, we work at a university that enthusiastically supports our scholarly work and collaboration. Vanderbilt University has been very good to us. Deans John Geer, Andre Christie-Mizell, and Kamal Saggi have all provided institutional opportunities for our research, writing, and intellectual development. And our colleagues in the Vanderbilt Philosophy Department have been insightful respondents and supporters. In particular, we wish to thank William James Booth, Matthew Congdon, Idit Dobbs-Weinstein, Lenn E. Goodman, Diana Heney, Michael Hodges, John Lachs, Karen Ng, Kelly Oliver, Paul Taylor, Jeffrey Tlumak, John Weymark, and Julian Wuerth. We also have had excellent students who were thinking along with us as we completed this book. Among these are Fiacha Heneghan, Tempest Henning, Alyssa Lowery, Lisa Madura, Takunda Matose, and Lyn Radke. Moreover, we are fortunate enough to belong to a rich and vibrant intellectual community of people thinking hard about many of the same issues that we regularly grapple with. We have learned a great deal from Jason Aleksander, Jody Azzouni, Heather Battaly, Erin Bradfield, Kimberley Brownlee, Steven Cahn, Gregg Caruso, John Patrick Casey, Caleb Clanton, Andrew Cling, Candice Delmas, Jeroen de Ridder, Ian Dove, Elizabeth Edenberg, David Estlund, Andrew Forcehimes, Gerald Gaus, David Godden, Sandy Goldberg, David Miguel Gray,

ACKNOWLEDGMENTS

Hannah Gunn, Michael Hannon, Michael Harbour, Nicole Hassoun, David Hildebrand, Michael Hoppman, Andrew Howat, Catherine Hundleby, Klemens Kappell, David Kaspar, Chris King, Holly Korbey, Helene Landemore, Michael Lynch, Mason Marshall, Amy McKiernan, Joshua Miller, Cheryl Misak, Jonathan Neufeld, C. Dutilh Novaes, John O'Connor, Jeanine Palomino, John Peterman, Yvonne Raley, Brian Ribeiro, Regina Rini, Allysson V.L. Rocha, Luke Semrau, Harvey Siegel, Walter Sinnott-Armstrong, William O. Stephens, Katharina Stevens, Alessandra Tanesini, Rob Tempio, Lawerence Torcello, Kevin Vallier, and Leif Wenar. We should hasten to add that many of the people we've thanked here should not be blamed for our views and errors, as many of the people we've thanked here have disagreed with us most forcefully.

1

Democracy in Dark Days

This is not another *how to save democracy* book. Perhaps you are familiar with that type of book – the author laments the decline of some democratic norm, intones gravely about where the current trajectory takes us, and then outlines a set of fixes. There is, unsurprisingly, a small industry of books that follow this formula. They sell. They function as a kind of self-help for the political class. Now, that's not a bad thing by any means, but we think there is a false premise behind it all. Democracy can't be fixed.

So this clearly isn't a book about how to save democracy. What is it, instead? Well, it's not a case *against democracy*, either. Just because democracy can't be fixed, it doesn't follow that we should do away with it. This is because doing away with democracy requires that we put something else in its place, something that there's sufficient reason to think is superior to democracy. But this comparative work is fraught. Notice that the relevant comparison is *not* between real-world democracy and some idealized nondemocratic alternative. Instead, the relevant comparison is between democracy as it presently functions and some envisioned alternative as it would function were it instated. When the comparison is performed properly, democracy comes out on top. So this isn't an anti-democracy book; we think there is no better political arrangement than democracy, even when it is functioning poorly.

This isn't a *saving democracy* book, and it's not a *down with democracy* book. So what is it? Well, it's complicated, but that's what happens when you ask tough questions that do not admit of simple answers. In fact, we hold that one of the problems with democracy is that it encourages citizens to expect there to be simple answers to complicated political questions. Hence the popularity of the two genres we have mentioned; the literature of both *saving democracy* and *down with democracy* is driven by the demand for easy answers.

Still, something should be said at the start about what this book is about. The view we will present can be sketched as follows. We understand democracy to be the proposal that a stable and decent political order can be sustained by equal citizens who nonetheless disagree, often sharply, about the precise shape their collective life should take. On this view, political disagreement among political equals is central to democracy. Disagreements of this kind are the engine of collective self-government. However, the practices associated with political disagreement and the freedoms guaranteed to citizens that enable them to engage in political argumentation – particularly, freedoms of conscience, expression, and association – create the conditions under which the democratic citizenry fractures into hostile and opposed factions. For reasons we will explain in these pages, political factions have a tendency to transform their members into polarized extremists who grow incapable of seeing their political opponents as fellow citizens. Yet maintaining a commitment to the political equality of our political opposition is the central demand of the democratic ethos, the ethos of the democratic citizen.

Note the tragic irony. Our enactment of democratic citizenship leads to the kind of polarization that dismantles our democratic capacities. We recognize the central democratic freedoms precisely because collective self-government among equals needs citizens to deliberate and argue together about matters of public concern. But in order to argue well together, citizens must be able to access and process the reasons and evidence that are relevant to their disputes; and they must *engage* with one another. The need to engage in argument with those with whom one disagrees prompts certain forms of democratic dysfunction. In particular, we will focus in this book on the ways in which the need to engage in such argument creates the occasion for *simulated* argument, mimicked political engagement. These are processes and practices that are designed to *look like* political argumentation among equal citizens that are in fact strategies for avoiding and shutting down such engagement. When authentic political argumentation is successfully shut down in this way, opposing factions polarize, democratic capacities are dismantled, and citizens become increasingly incapable of the real thing. Democracy thus is undermined from within.

It's important to emphasize that this dysfunction is a *product of democracy*, not the work of some alien and counter-democratic political ideal. And it is not an accidental product of democracy. It is a product of democracies as democracies. The fact is that we factionalize and polarize as a consequence of sincerely trying to enact democratic citizenship properly. It's not a fact of disproportionate wealth distributions or caused by racism or regionalism, though these factors certainly hasten it. No, it's a feature of democracies as democracies, because this kind of disagreement is central to the democratic project, and the pathologies of political argument are consequences of democratic freedoms. This is why democracy cannot be saved, at least not in the way that animates much of the current literature devoted to saving it. Fractious disagreement is an essential cog in the machinery of democratic politics. Fixing democracy cannot be a matter of quelling or sidelining our political disagreements.

A political order without real disagreement and disputes in which participants get heated is no democracy at all. The trick is to find a way to conduct disputes of that kind while also sustaining our respect for the political equality of our opposition. Although we employ the term advisedly, we claim here that the task is to formulate a workable conception of *civil* political disagreement. More on that term shortly. But, again, however, this is not a promise of *saving* democracy, but of *managing the symptoms* of its core problem.

Civility and the Owl of Minerva Problem

We actually agree with the folks who write those *how to save democracy* books, at least about one thing: contemporary democracies are failing to handle political disagreement properly. Political divisions and antagonisms have reached such a pitch that citizens indeed find it difficult to see why their political opponents are their equals. They are growing increasingly inclined to regard those with whom they disagree over politics to be not merely incorrect, but depraved, dangerous, and threatening to democracy itself.

It seems that if the problem lies with the level of antagonism citizens have toward their political opposition, there should be a fix. But we have already indicated that we think there is no fix. Why? Again, our answer is complicated, and the central task of this book is to spell out the problem we find with reparative strategies. Here's a thumbnail version. Our attempts to correct democratic practice requires creating new rules and norms for democratic citizens to follow, or perhaps reminding citizens of rules that they implicitly endorse and wish we all could follow. However, partisan divisions are at present so severe that any such proposal will be received by some significant segment of the citizenry as biased against their own political allegiances; thus, our strategies of correction are transformed into tools of partisan attack. Any tools we might devise for fixing democracy will become additional instruments for its dysfunction.

Part of the trouble is that we are trying to understand something while we are doing it, and the resulting theorizing and prescriptions that follow from that effort in turn change what we are aiming to understand. Accordingly, our explanations are always at least one step behind the phenomenon to be explained. We call this *The Owl of Minerva Problem*. The mythological Owl of Minerva brings understanding, but it flies only at dusk, after the dust has settled. So our understanding of democratic argumentation applies only in retrospect, because once we make that understanding public, we change the practice of democratic argumentation.

To grasp this, think of all the ways that "tone policing" in the name of civility has become a way of attacking the other side for not adopting the correct tone. A norm is identified for democratic arguers to embrace in conducting their disputes, but then that very norm itself becomes a tool for expressing one's contempt for the other side. We dismiss the other side's views by impugning the ways in which they are expressed. Think of all the times that, in a heated exchange, the tone with which one side puts their point becomes the topic of discussion, a stand-in for their view. Now, we have two disagreements: what we'd originally disagreed about, and also how we've been managing that disagreement. Anyone who's been to family therapy or taken part in team-building exercises can recognize that the tools of these ways of bringing us together can be turned into new and cruel weapons. In this way, the norm is turned against itself: the attempt to make explicit a way to get along becomes a tool for *not* getting along. This point generalizes: certain kinds of incivility are possible only once we've tried to model civility. That's the Owl of Minerva Problem in a nutshell.

Hence a recurring theme of this book: civility produces its own discontent. Political argument, even when civil, has challenges that branch out to our larger culture and that loop back on themselves. Our attempts to conduct ourselves properly amidst political disagreement create the possibility for new modes of incivility, precisely by way of the norms they instantiate. Notice that this phenomenon is at work in the case of the very concept of civility. Here's how. You have political views, and lots of other citizens in your city and country have political views as well. Many of them have political views that are inconsistent with your own. Moreover, many of those folks have views you think are not only wrong, but benighted or abhorrent, and in any case not worthy of serious consideration or respect. And they think the same of you and your views: they see you as adhering to political ideas that are ridiculous and ignorant. But here's the deal with democracy: our commitment to collective self-government among political equals means that sometimes these other folks will get their way, and the government will shape policy in light of their views. And, although democracy permits you to enact your opposition to the prevailing policies in various ways, you still have to live with the fact that your side lost and the other side won. For the time being, and of course within the standard constitutional constraints, your political opponents get to decide how things will go. That's simply how democracy works. Equal citizens have equal input into the decision-making process, and we all abide by the results of that process. After all, you expect your opponents to live with it when your views prevail, so you have to do the same. That's largely what political equality is.

But in cases where the political stakes are high, many democratic citizens entertain the following background thought. Maybe there are views that are so wrong, so abhorrent and foolish, that holding them disqualifies a person for democratic citizenship. Surely there are views of this kind; they are views that are themselves inconsistent with democracy and its commitment to the political equality of all citizens. Managing citizens who adopt such views is a special problem for democratic theory that we cannot address in this book. The trouble is that factionalized and polarized citizens begin to regard *any* deviation from their own preferred political position as tantamount to adopting an *intolerable* view. Thus they come to see anyone who is not a fellow partisan as not only *incapable* of democratic citizenship, but a *threat* to democracy itself.

What we will be calling civility is a set of norms that enable citizens to manage their political disagreements, even in cases where the stakes are high. Civility in general is the disposition to regard fellow citizens as politically equal partners in collective government even when they hold political views that you regard as fundamentally mistaken, injudicious, and even reckless. However, civility is not *capitulation*. And it needn't mean social etiquette, like conversation with soft tones and maintaining a veneer of niceness. Rather, civility as we understand it in this book is composed of the dispositions needed to disagree well even when disagreeing vehemently, to hear each other's reasons, make the stakes clear, and look at the various positives and negatives in ways that get to the bottom of the matter. Civility is a commitment to norms of proper argument.

Now, if civility is a matter of good argument, then logic has a political edge. Our examples of arguments that live up to these norms and those that break them will be drawn from politics in the United States – we are writing about the democratic environment that we know best. But we think that the cases are generalizable. The terms and trends of logic and critical exchange show up in political debates well beyond America – "fake news" and "whataboutery" are now global terms. Our overall objective in these pages is to make a case for ways to repair our arguments piece by piece, and repair our culture of civil exchange in the process. Thus, this is not a recipe for fixing or saving democracy, but rather a method for managing the vices that democratic politics engenders. It is an outline of the work that democracy requires of us.

2

Civility and Its Discontents

Democracy is hard to love. It's noisy, contentious, frustrating, and inefficient. It involves meetings, caucuses, and committees. There's a seemingly endless procession of polls, surveys, campaigns, and speeches. Sometimes democracy calls on us to canvass, demonstrate, and protest. More than this, democracy is also a suspicious moral proposal. It is the thesis that you may be required to live according to rules that you reject, simply because they are favored by others. Further, democracy is the claim that you may be rightfully forced to live according to rules that are supported only by others who are demonstrably ignorant, misinformed, deluded, corrupt, irrational, or worse. Democracy apportions equal political power to its citizens, regardless of their ability to wield it responsibly. Plato famously argued that as in any society there will be very few people who are wise, democracy is simply the rule of the foolish. What could be worse?

Nonetheless we tend to embrace democracy emphatically. But why? Consider Winston Churchill's famous rationale: despite all of democracy's flaws, every other form of government that has been tried is far worse. That rings true enough. But there's less to this argument than meets the eye. We tend to see democracy as a supreme social good, rather than as merely the least bad in a collection of terrible alternatives. We are inclined to regard democracy as the best political system there could be. Thus we treat it as something to be cultivated, expanded, promoted, exported, and protected. Are these attitudes warranted? What's so great about democracy?

Democracy as a Society of Equals

In order to address this question, we need to take a step back. Democracy is many things. It's a form of constitutional republicanism in which all citizens are ruled not by government but by laws, a system of popular government, a procedure for collective decision, a method for electing public officials, a collection of fair processes by which conflicts among competing preferences are domesticated, a means for creating social stability, and so on. But underneath all these common ways of defining democracy rests its fundamental commitment to the moral ideal of collective self-government among *political equals*. This commitment to the political equality of citizens is what explains the familiar mechanisms of democratic government. Our elections, representative bodies, constitutions, and systems of law and rights are intended to preserve individual political equality in the midst of large-scale government. Absent the presumption of political equality, much of what goes on in a democracy would be difficult to explain. Why else would we bother with all of the institutional inefficiency, the collective irrationality, and the *noise* of democracy, but for the commitment to the idea that government must be of, for, and by the People, understood as political equals?

Even though democracy is hard to love, it is nonetheless beloved because it is a system of politics explicitly committed to our status as equals. To be clear, that commitment to equality does not involve the claim that everyone is the same, or equally good. Democratic equality rather amounts to the idea that, as far as politics goes, no one is another's subordinate, superior, servant, or boss. In a democracy, no single person simply gets to call the shots for the rest of us. The political rules we live by are in some sense products of our collective political will. Although the function of government requires that certain people occupy *offices* that give them special power to do things like make laws, set policies, and give orders, that power is always constrained and the office holders are accountable to the citizens over whom their power is exercised. In a democracy, we collectively call our own shots.

Now, if everyone agreed about which shots to call, there would be no need for democracy, or any form of politics at all. But, as we all know, politics is fraught with disagreement. And some of this disagreement comes to more than mere foot stomping and horse-trading. That is, political disagreement is not confined to instances where different people merely want different things and have to strike a bargain. Political disagreement often runs deeper than this. It frequently involves conflicting judgments of justice, meaning, and value, differences among citizens concerning what we, collectively, *ought to do*. The familiar architecture of the democratic decision-making process – open elections, equal voting, and majority rule – serves to ensure that collective political decisions can be made in a way that each citizen can regard as fair, despite their ongoing disagreements. Recognizing that, in a society of political equals, no one person can simply call the shots for everybody else, democracy provides a system for collective decision-making in which, although we are sometimes required to abide by rules and decisions that we oppose, no one is rendered a subordinate, a mere subject of another's will.

Three related points follow. First, democracy is never simply majority rule. Rather, democracy is a system of majority rule *constrained* by a constitution that identifies individual rights. These rights both recognize and protect each individual's status as a political equal. Thus, in a democracy, there are some things that not even a vast majority of one's fellow citizens can accomplish politically. Second, in a democracy, even when your side loses the election, you are never required simply to *acquiesce* in the outcome. You are permitted – and perhaps expected – to continue campaigning, objecting, and pressing for change after the votes have been counted. There's always the next election, democratic collective decisions are revisable, and your rights guarantee that you still have an equal say. Third, in a democracy, part of what makes political power consistent with the political equality of the citizens is that democratic processes allow citizens to hold power *accountable*. Democracy calls on its citizens to hold office holders *responsible* for our collective life. Consequently, our role as citizens carries the duty to *participate* in the activities of self-government. In this way, political critique, challenge, resistance, and activism are all part of democracy.

When cast in this light, our enthusiasm for democracy is easier to understand. For all of its flaws, democracy is the proposal that we each are entitled to an equal say in directing our collective life. No one simply gets to boss everyone else around. Despite vast differences in knowledge, experience, moral character, talent, and ambition, we are in matters of politics one another's equals. As citizens, we look each other in the eye. And in looking each other in the eye, we keep government under our joint scrutiny and in check. Far from being merely the least bad, democracy turns out to be positively *dignifying*. Accordingly, democracy is not only beloved. It is eminently *lovable*, deserving of our attachment to it.

Political Disagreement among Equals

In formulating this image of democracy, we have admittedly focused on it as an *ideal*. Our image of a society of equal citizens engaging in the activities of collective self-government is, after all, the *aspiration* of democracy, what democracy strives to be. We are well aware that real-world democracy falls far short of the ideal, and this book is devoted to identifying and examining some of the causes of its failures. Still, in diagnosing real-world democracy's shortcomings, we mustn't lose sight of the fact that, even in the ideal, democracy is a system of politics based in the premise that equal citizens are bound to disagree, sometimes profoundly, about what is good. Such disagreement is, after all, the upshot of our political equality. That's an important thing to remember about this ideal notion of democracy – central to it, even in the ideal form, is the notion that free and equal citizens will have significant disagreements and, because they are equals, they can't just boss each other around. And the democratic ideal is that, when no one person simply gets to call the shots for everyone else, each citizen has a duty to participate in collective self-government. This means that citizens will exercise their own judgment about the shape of collective political life, and this will naturally lead to disagreement among citizens. Accordingly, real-world political conflict, rancor, and disputation are not necessarily failures of democracy; they are *exercises* of democracy. Even in the ideal form, democracy is fractious.

We might say that disagreement is at the heart of democracy, both in the real world and as an ideal. Democracy is the proposal that a morally decent and socially stable collective life is possible among political equals who do not agree fully about how they should live together.

Now, disagreement in general presents problems. When we disagree with each other, we can't get along, our plans get complicated, and sometimes even ruined. Disagreement also can escalate hostility, threaten friendships, breed contempt, and tear people apart. What's more, where there's disagreement there is also the acknowledgment that at least one party to the dispute must be wrong, and so, if the disagreement is pursued and resolved, someone will have to change their mind. We tend to not like changing our mind, and so earnest disagreement can prove psychologically costly. Even at is best, disagreement is risky.

Yet political disagreement – disagreement about the structure and aims of our collective life – presents an additional and distinctive problem, and it takes a little work to identify what it is. To begin, recall that political disagreements tend to have a certain *depth* in that they invoke conflicting judgments of value and meaning, views about what is good with respect to our collective life. Moreover, the *stakes* in such disagreements are frequently morally *high* in that the parties involved tend to see their own prevailing view as necessary for justice. Consequently, political disagreement often is engaged in among parties who see the opposition's view as not merely flawed, inadequate, or suboptimal, but as positively wrong, possibly intolerable, and potentially disastrous. Putting these together, we can say that political disagreements are often engaged in among citizens who have a certain *investment* in seeing their own view prevail.

Next, remember that in a democracy, political disagreements always take place among political *equals*. No one simply gets to browbeat, harangue, lecture, or dictate to their fellow citizens – at least not about the political matters that face democratic decision-making. Rather, in interactions with our fellow citizens, we must manifest a due respect for their political equality. Even when we disagree with our fellow citizens about matters in which we are deeply invested, and even when we are inclined to regard our fellow citizens as invested in manifestly unacceptable alternative positions, we nonetheless must sustain our commitment to their political standing as our equals.

Maintaining this commitment often proves difficult, especially given that political disagreements frequently get heated. When we disagree over matters in which we are invested, it is all too easy to tar the opposing side with being depraved, incompetent, helplessly benighted, and incapable. When we regard others in this way, we grow to see them as something less than our political equals. They begin to appear to us as misguided underlings in need of a lesson, or, worse still, mere obstacles to be surmounted. Either way, we begin to abandon our commitment to their equality. If left unchecked, we begin to wonder why our political rivals are entitled to an equal say. In this way, although disagreement is central to the democratic ideal, it can thwart our fundamental moral commitment to the political equality of our fellow citizens. In short, democracy runs on political disagreement, but when political disagreement is poorly conducted, it can unravel democracy.

Hence the problem of political disagreement: how can we engage in *real* disagreement in ways that nevertheless manifest due respect for one another's political equality? In order to address this problem, we need to devise an *ethos* that could govern political disagreements among citizens. To repeat, the rules of this *ethos* must permit *real* disagreement among citizens; we make no progress by simply stipulating that democratic citizens must always show deference to the majority, or decline to criticize those in power. Yet, as the function of this ethos is to preserve and manifest respect for the political equality of all citizens amidst real political disagreements, it must take the form of a moral requirement. That is, the norms governing political disagreement among democratic citizens must be such that, when someone violates them, she not only fails at appropriate engagement, she also fails at citizenship. We also can say that when a citizen exhibits a stable disposition to abide by democratic ethos in contexts of political disagreement, she thereby manifests civic virtue, the kind of virtue appropriate for a democratic citizen.

Civility in Political Disagreement

Our aim in this book is to identify the nature of proper political disagreement among democratic citizens. For simplicity's sake, we will refer to the dispositions appropriate for democratic citizens engaged in political disagreement as the virtues of *civility*. Often, we will talk about *civil political disagreement*; sometimes we refer simply to *civility*. We will occasionally talk of a citizen's *duty of civility*, which is the duty to cultivate and exhibit civility in contexts of political disagreement. We employ the term *civility* with some degree of trepidation, as it is freighted with associations that we reject. So a few preliminary marks about the term are in order.

As commonly used in talking about politics, the term *civility* denotes a mild or accommodating mode of behavior, and this includes a posture of politeness and a pacifying or gentle tone of voice. Civility in this sense is inconsistent with heated and exercised argumentation, loud speech, and expressions of antagonism of any kind. Accordingly, civility has been subjected to a good deal of forceful criticism among political thinkers. Taken in its usual sense, civility unduly favors the status quo by placing heavy burdens on those who feel most aggrieved by the way things are, and then privileges those who are already advantaged by the kind of upbringing and education that enables them to sustain a calm demeanor and tone of voice amidst conflict. Indeed, it is common among feminist political theorists to reject appeals to civility as inherently patriarchal, as condemning the excitability and emotionality that traditionally has been associated with women.

These objections to civility strike us as correct. And yet our view is that democratic citizens have a duty of civility when engaging in political disagreement. The apparent contradiction is dispelled by the fact that we use the term civility in a different sense than the one that is targeted in these criticisms. We do not contend that proper democratic disagreement requires citizens to always maintain a posture of calmness or politeness, or a pacifying and gentle tone of voice. Civil political disagreement is, after all, real *disagreement*. And so the heat and passion of disputes over things that matter are consistent with the kind of civility we are calling for. Citizens can be civil and yet raise their voices, engage in sharp or biting rhetoric, and adopt an antagonist posture toward others. Civility is a set of dispositions we bring to contexts of disagreement; it is not a requirement for resignation or conciliation. It's not about being nice, it's about disagreeing and arguing properly.

To be sure, the central aim of this book is to present a workable conception of civility. But to put things very roughly, *civility* is that set of dispositions that enable citizens to manifest their commitment to the political equality of their political opponents amidst political disagreement over matters in which they are invested. In part, civility is set of attitudes associated with engaging earnestly and fairly with the arguments and perspectives presented by one's opponents. In political argument, civility involves engaging with one's interlocutor's actual views rather than with convenient distortions of them, honestly addressing their reasons, declining to take cheap shots, and so on. Civility is also readiness to offer to one's interlocutors in political disagreement reasons and arguments that one sincerely believes they could appreciate the force of. That is, when disagreeing civilly, interlocutors actually *address* each other; they do not use the argumentative interaction as merely a tactical contest to stump or "own" a critic. Finally, when political disagreement is civil, interlocutors aspire not only to convince others of the correctness of their own position, they also seek to deepen everyone's *comprehension* of the matter in dispute. This means that when arguing civilly, disputants do not seek merely to win converts, and they do not use the exchange as an occasion simply to mug to an audience of sympathetic onlookers.

In short, civility in the sense we will use it here names the collection of tendencies that are necessary for political disagreement to yield enhanced *understanding* of the point in dispute, even if not agreement. Again, civility in this sense is obviously consistent with raising one's voice, offering sharp rebuttals to one's critics, and adopting a combative tone. In order to be civil, one needn't be soft-spoken, calm, or resigning; one needs rather to argue honestly.

The Demands of Civility

Civility is nonetheless demanding. It may seem to be so demanding that no actual democratic citizen would even try to adhere to its requirements. And even if some democratic citizens do take up the challenge of civil political disagreement, it's obvious that many more will not, and civility has value for democracy only if it is widespread among political disputants. So why bother?

This is a serious challenge, and this entire book is an attempt to meet it. However, we can bring this chapter to a close with the following preliminary response.

An intriguing phenomenon in contemporary political discourse supplies the basis for much of our inquiry. Political communication is almost exclusively conducted by means of purported debate among people with different views; cable news is dominated by programming that features panel discussion among experts who disagree; and politics online largely consists of threads, comments boards, and pile-ons, in which participants constantly present themselves as devoted to facts, reason, and logic. In short, our political discourse is almost entirely argument-based, and the vast majority of participants explicitly extoll the virtue of honest and earnest engagement that we have identified as civility.

Yet here's the intrigue. Although the dominant *images* of our politics are more dressed in the attire of civility (in the sense depicted above), our actual politics has become increasingly *tribal* – devoted to circle-the-wagons campaigns, celebrity spokespersons, and the on-point messaging of carefully curated and audience-tested party lines. Citizens seem increasingly unable to grasp the perspectives of those with whom they politically disagree, and yet they are fervently convinced that they need to be engaged in argument all the time. In short, as appeals to reason, argument, and evidence become more common in political communication, our capacity to actually *disagree and argue* – to respond to criticisms and objections, to address considerations that countervail our views, and to identify precisely where we think our opponents have erred – has significantly deteriorated. And here's a notable irony: everyone seems to know this and bemoan it.

We draw from this the hypothesis that democratic citizens are already committed to what we have called civility. They indeed embrace the ideals of proper political argumentation among political equals. And, moreover, they are devoted to trying to participate civilly in the kind of political disagreement that is called for by democracy. Yet their efforts are being somehow thwarted. This book argues that clever *simulations* of civil disagreement are misdirecting our democratic aspirations. Citizens already embrace the proper *ethos*, and they are prepared to put in the effort required for civil political disagreement. However, they are surrounded by distortions of civility: sites of market-tested and targeted *pantomimes* of democratic engagement. Accordingly, citizens tend to get their view of their political opposition not from actual engagement, but from media outlets designed to appeal to those who share their political views. They learn about the other side from commercial enterprises marketing to their own side; unsurprisingly, citizens come to embrace distorted and skewed views of their political rivals. With such distortions in place, efforts at civil engagement will naturally fail. But they will fail in a way that the participants will see as *confirming* their views of the other side. Eventually, participants on all sides come to regard civil disagreement as a pointless endeavor, given the irrationality and depravity of those with whom they disagree. Our democratic aspirations are thus undermined, but from the inside. Civility is turned against itself; it breeds its own discontent.

Hence, our task in the following chapters is not to make a case for civility. Nor need we present a defense of democracy as involving an ethos of civility. Our readers already take themselves to be committed to the view that democracy requires citizens to engage in civil political debate. There's no doubt about that. What's more, our readers believe themselves to be proficient at civility. They see the troubles with public discourse as emerging mainly from the public vices of those on the other side. Our task instead is to propose a way of diagnosing the ways in which civility breaks down, even among citizens sincerely committed to it.

3

Evaluating Argument

In Chapter 1, we showed that political disagreement is central to democracy, both as an ideal and in real-world practice. We also suggested that democratic citizens generally embrace the idea that it is part of their civic duty to engage together in civil disagreement. This explains why our news programs are saturated with political debate and discussion panels. In a democracy, political disagreement is simply what we do in our role as citizens. However, that we are generally inclined to both engage in and value civil political disagreement does not mean that we are adept at it. In order to disagree civilly, we need to argue well. And in order to argue well, we need to develop methods for evaluating argument.

Often, we proceed as if the evaluation of an argument is simply a matter of assessing its conclusion. In fact, a good deal of our popular political discourse proceeds as if it were the case that good argument simply is a matter of standing firm on your favored position. But this can't be correct. Someone can propose terrible reasons for a conclusion that we agree with, just as another person can present us with a cogent case for a conclusion we reject. Evaluating an argument is different from deciding whether to accept or reject a claim, and it's different from being steadfast in affirming a position. In order to get a better feel for what's required, we need to begin from square one.

Argumentation and Its Values

Argumentation is the term used to denote the *activity* of arguing with a real interlocutor, in real time, over claims that are actually in dispute. When argumentation is properly conducted, the parties involved exchange arguments, objections, criticisms, and rejoinders, all aimed at discerning the truth (or at least what one would be most justified in accepting as true). To be sure, argumentation does not always result in consensus among disputants; even when argumentation is impeccably conducted, disagreement can persist. But this is no strike against argumentation. This is for a few reasons. First, the open exchange of reasons, evidence, and criticism is, after all, the best means we have for rationally resolving disputes; there is no alternative to argumentation that doesn't have a far worse track record when it comes to addressing disputes rationally. Furthermore, even when argumentation does not dispel disagreement, it nonetheless can provide disputants with a firmer grasp of precisely where they differ. This is important because, as John Stuart Mill famously observed, understanding the views of one's critics is an essential element of understanding one's own position.

At any rate, people aspire to form and maintain true beliefs and eschew false beliefs. The central way in which they enact this aspiration is by arguing with each other. Alas, the pitfalls of human reasoning are abundant, and there is rightly a substantial academic industry devoted to identifying, studying, and cataloguing them. What is important to emphasize here is that detecting argumentative pitfalls is itself part of the activity of argumentation. Arguing involves more than the clash of claims about how things stand in the world; it also requires us to evaluate our performance as arguers. Indeed, arguing involves arguing about arguing.

Thus, in order to argue well, we must devise a vocabulary for talking about and evaluating arguments. That is, we need to be able to talk about something whether or not we accept what an interlocutor has claimed. We need to be able to assess how our interlocutor's statements are *related* to each other. Does one speaker's claim that Adolf Hitler was a vegetarian *support* her conclusion that it's not immoral to eat meat? Is another person's reason for opposing capital punishment *consistent* with his stance on abortion? Does the president's pronouncement on immigration restrictions *contradict* his statements about the free market? Note that these questions have nothing do with whether one ought to adopt any particular position with respect to vegetarianism, capital punishment, or immigration. They're entirely about how some specific arguer's claims are related.

When we move from the level of assessing an interlocutor's claims to assessing the logical relations between them, we are still in the business of assessing what the interlocutor has said. When someone asserts two clams that are *inconsistent*, we know that at least one of them must be false. Thus, if the first claim was proposed as evidence for the second, we know that the speaker has failed to make her case. That does not prove that the second of her two claims is false, but only that she failed to provide good reason to adopt it as true. We can capture this more generally by saying that when one proposes an argument, one both asserts a conclusion that one takes to be true, and tries to display the *reason* why the conclusion is true. But the truth of a statement and the strength of reason why it should be accepted as true are different things.

In argumentation, then, one does not merely react disapprovingly to one's interlocutor's views; one must also diagnose her errors in arriving at those claims or commending them to you. Accordingly, a robust, though not entirely well-regimented, diagnostic idiom has developed for identifying, classifying, and correcting errors in real-time reasoning. "Critical thinking" textbooks are filled with such analyses. But we needn't look to academic literature to find examples of a diagnostic vocabulary for argumentation. One can look directly to the arena of political disagreement. The popular concepts of "spin," "bias," "false equivalence," "talking points," "bullshit," "cherry-picking," "truthiness," "dog-whistle," "bluster," "derp," and "fake news" function in the vernacular as tools with which political arguers charge each other with argumentative failure and wrongdoing.

To be sure, these are the names of genuine argumentative errors. When an interlocutor responds to a criticism by simply repeating lines from his prefabricated script, he has failed at argumentation. When someone imports the noncontroversial conclusion from her reasoning about one case into her reasoning about another case that is not relevantly similar, she has, indeed, made a mistake of faulty analogy, a "false equivalence." The same goes for those who argue on the basis of premises that contain conveniently skewed or incomplete data, and those whose arguments rely on key terms being interpreted in idiosyncratic ways that are common only among those who already accept their conclusions. One might say that the very fact that we have such robust ways of talking about argumentative failure speaks to the high degree of importance we place on arguing well.

This observation – that our vocabulary of criticism of argument indicates that we in fact value good argument – is not insignificant. Think of any domain of activity around which there has emerged a vocabulary of correction. That vocabulary exists for the sake of maintaining and enforcing that set of norms we think those activities should embody; the vocabulary exists because we *care* about the activities and want them to go well rather than badly. And so many sports have not only fouls, but informal rules of play that are assessed as legal but unsporting. Soccer, for example, has rules and mandated penalties for breaking them (e.g., field players may not touch the ball with their hands in the run of play, and the other team is given a free kick when someone breaks the rule). And there are gestures one makes in the spirit of the game that are not mandated by the rules. For example, if a player on one team is injured but play continues, the opposing team may stop play by kicking the ball out of bounds so that the teams can play at even numbers. The point is that we have these rules, both formal and informal, because we value these practices – we care about them, encourage excellence in them by cultivating the best play and discouraging disruptive infractions.

Because we call fouls and have these informal norms, we have an idea of what a good game looks like. The same goes for argument. We have a rich vocabulary of fallacies and argumentative missteps because we value argument and its competent performance, and we have a pretty good idea of what that looks like. The key is that we share that vocabulary, we teach it to each other, and we hold one another to the standards it sets. We do this so we can create a community that not only values good argument, but also mutually enforces its norms.

Abuses of Argumentation

Here are our results thus far. Disagreement is central to democracy. In order to fulfill our duties as democratic citizens, we need to engage in civil political disagreement, disagreement that manifests our political equality amidst our conflict. Civil political disagreement is built on proper argumentation – well-ordered rational exchange between interlocutors. Proper argumentation is a collective enterprise that in part requires interlocutors to assess each other's argumentative performance. Disagreeing well therefore involves an earnest attempt to *diagnose* the disagreement, to find its root, to explain why dissensus persists. Consequently, we need a vocabulary with which we can assess and criticize each other's argumentative performance.

However, the need to diagnose others' performance in argumentation itself provides occasions for abuse. Wrongly criticizing another's argumentative performance is *itself* an argumentative failure. In its most overt manifestations, misplaced criticism of one's interlocutor's performance is worse than an argumentative error; it is a covert attempt to derail argumentation from within. The rules for keeping discourse on the straight and narrow have derailed it. Here, too, there is need for a diagnostic vocabulary. Some of the more familiar informal fallacies call out improper treatment of one's interlocutor: the *straw man*, the *ad hominem*, and *well-poisoning*. In the case of the straw man, one misrepresents the interlocutor's claims or arguments as far weaker than they actually are, and then criticizes the flimsy misrepresentation. Even if the criticism of the case at hand is correct, the opposition's actual views are not given any attention, and one acts as though the discussion is over. In the case of *ad hominem* abuse, one simply makes the case against *the person* on the other side – that they have some (purported) vice, or that they are unpopular, and then one leaves the reactions of contempt for the person to do the work of forcing listeners to recoil from the things they say. And finally, with well-poisoning, one frames one's opponents in a such a way that, before they even speak, the listening audience cannot trust them or take them seriously. These are not simple errors of *reasoning*, but they are failures of *argumentation*. They are strategies for rendering one's opposition unhearable. That's a way of disregarding or repudiating their equality.

The key is that with each of these charges of breaking the rules of argument, there comes a *burden of proof*. That is, if one arguer charges another with having *erected a straw man*, that arguer herself must show that there is a significant difference between the views she holds and the ones criticized by her interlocutor. The same goes for *ad hominem* abuse – if you accuse another arguer of using the *ad hominem* against you, you have to show not only that they said harsh things about your character that had nothing to do with the matter in dispute, but that they implied that you were wrong because of these alleged character flaws. And the same with well-poisoning, too. The point is that in all these cases of calling foul in argument, we are required to give arguments about the arguments given. This is because, in argumentation, we are all both the players and referees. And here is where the abuse arises – we don't just want to argue well, we want to be able to police our performances in a way that's open to all to inspect and endorse. And so bad play can happen if we break the rules, but it can also happen if we are bad at identifying infractions, or if we systematically misidentify infractions for our own benefit. Consider the possibility of a person you're arguing with who, every time you show up with a criticism, accuses you of constructing a straw man of their view. Or consider the idea of another person who argues with you about a policy, and any implication that their views on the policy would yield immoral action or would be callous is met with the charge that you are arguing *ad hominem*. The tools for improved critical discussion have just become impediments to it. That's really bad news, right? The tools for fixing argument have become tools for a unique kind of pathology.

In contemporary political debate across the spectrum of opinion, especially at the national level, these fallacy forms are increasingly prevalent. Not only do people commit the fallacies, but they regularly call each other out for them. Perhaps this is because in high-stakes political argumentation, the political calculation is that the need to sway voters far outweighs the prerogative to argue well. There's an irony, however, in the fact that voters are best swayed *by what can be made to look like* proper argument. Although citizens, politicians, and pundits alike all agree that what is commonly presented as political argumentation is at best a mimic and a marketing strategy, no candidate dares to give up the pantomime. They must uphold the *appearance* of argumentation, while they in fact simply seek to dismiss, insult, denigrate, and defuse their opposition. And we all recognize that, and so, it's to their advantage to use the vocabulary of criticism to give themselves the veneer of being the ones who genuinely care for argument.

The result, then, is that in political disagreement our robust idiom for diagnosing argumentative failures is misdirected toward defaming opponents and effectively ignoring their criticisms. Once again, our commitment to civil political disagreement is turned against itself, put in the service of its opposite. The surest sign of this transformation is that our diagnostic vocabulary about argumentative performance among interlocutors now functions as an idiom for dismissing opponent's views. "Bias," "spin," "slant," and the like are now used to smear views and their proponents, rather than to describe the quality and character of the support an interlocutor has offered for her view. To accuse someone of spouting "talking points" or "politicizing" an event is now simply to say that she's voicing a view that one opposes. The charge of arguing from a "false equivalence" now functions simply as the claim that one's interlocutor is saying something disagreeable.

One way to characterize this transformation is to say that our second-order vocabulary for discussing the logical *relations* between our interlocutors' claims has been downgraded into a first-order vocabulary for signaling our rejection of their claims and a way of rebuffing their attempts at critical exchange. This is why no one ever asserts that one's *allies* have "talking points," or engage in "spin." Similarly, no one describes an erroneous news story that supports one's side as "fake news."

This descent of the diagnostic idiom is bad news for democracy. We saw earlier that civil political disagreement requires that we argue well. And arguing well involves properly evaluating one another's performance in argumentation. But evaluations of that kind need to be distinct from our assessments of our interlocutors' claims. After all, it is only in virtue of our capacity to keep our substantive disagreements distinct from our assessments of each other's arguments that we can keep political disagreement civil. To put the point simplistically, we can regard our political opponents as our equals only if we can sustain the distinction between seeing them as *wrong* and seeing them as *stupid, incompetent,* and *cognitively depraved.* The collapsing of the second-order vocabulary for evaluating argumentative performances into the first-order idiom for rejecting and dismissing our opponent's claims undermines this crucial distinction. Thus, it disables our capacity for civil political disagreement. And as the capacity for civility fades, so does our democracy.

4

Our Polarization Problem

The preceding chapter charted the troubling descent of our robust second-order vocabulary for evaluating argumentative performance into the first-order idiom for rebuffing our opponents' views. We argued there that democracy needs citizens to engage in civil political disagreement, and civility depends on our being able to sustain the distinction between the evaluation of our interlocutors' argumentative performances and their substantive political views. The collapsing of the second-order evaluative vocabulary erases this distinction; it makes it difficult to see how sometimes our political opponents have good reasons for their views. And so, with the collapse of the second-order vocabulary, citizens come to regard their political opponents as not only wrong, but cognitively depraved. It's not easy to see those whom one regards as depraved as one's equals, and so the descent of the second-order vocabulary into the first-order serves to dismantle the democratic ethos. In order to satisfy our duty of civility, we need to keep our substantive political opinions distinct from the norms and standards that we use when assessing argumentative performances.

Alas, there's more bad news. Once citizens have grown accustomed to regarding their political opponents as depraved and incompetent rather than as merely mistaken, they will become increasingly disinclined to interact with anyone who is not just like themselves.

To be sure, democratic citizens enjoy freedom of association, and democratic politics depends upon citizens' ability to form likeminded coalitions devoted to particular policies and platforms. But when such groups are formed among likeminded citizens who are also convinced that anyone outside the group is therefore depraved and incapable of democratic citizenship, distinctive pathologies emerge, leading to the further dismantling of our democratic capacities. More specifically, these conditions are ripe for a phenomenon known as *belief polarization*.

Two Kinds of Polarization

Popular political commentary from across the spectrum is replete with warnings about social "bubbles," "silos," and "echo chambers." These are said to produce "closure," "groupthink," and an "alternate reality." In turn, these forces result in the dysfunction of *polarization*, a condition where political officials and ordinary citizens are so deeply divided that there is no basis for compromise or even productive communication among them.

That polarization is politically dysfunctional might seem obvious. Where polarization prevails, the ground for compromise recedes, and so politics becomes a series of standoffs and bottlenecks. Yet politics still needs to get done. Under these conditions, democracy therefore devolves into a numbers game of begrudging truces and strained compromises, resembling nothing like self-government among politically equal citizens. And it's important to note that, in the midst of these polarized conditions, no one is happy about it – bemoaning the polarized state of our discourse seems to be the only thing the disparate sides share in common.

It is helpful to distinguish two different kinds of polarization: *political* and *belief*. Political polarization refers to various ways of measuring the *distance* between political rivals. This distance can be conceived in terms of policy and platform divides or else in terms of interparty antipathy. Of course, these two metrics are rather different and needn't go together. In fact, some data suggest that interparty antipathy has intensified in recent years despite there being no similar increase of partisan divisions at the level of policies and platforms. But in any case, where political polarization prevails, the common ground among opposing parties falls away, resulting in political deadlock.

Belief polarization refers to a phenomenon to which we are all subject. A series of studies conducted over several decades shows that interactions with likeminded others transforms us into more extreme versions of ourselves. This research demonstrates that when we talk only to others who share our views, we each come to hold more extreme versions of those views. Notice that belief polarization is a different *kind* of phenomenon from political polarization; whereas the latter is a metric of the ideological distance *between* opposing political groups, the former has to do with ideological shifts *within* likeminded groups.

Consider some examples of belief polarization. One of the earliest experiments involved a group of Michigan high-schoolers. After being sorted according to their antecedently expressed level of racial prejudice, likeminded groups then were tasked with discussing several issues concerning race in the United States, including the question of whether racism is the cause of the socioeconomic disadvantages faced by African Americans. Following the conversations with their respective groups of likeminded others, those who antecedently showed a high level of racial prejudice came to embrace more ardently the view that racism is *not* responsible for the disadvantages faced by African Americans, while those antecedently disposed toward low levels of racial prejudice grew more accepting of the view that racism is the cause of such disadvantages. Once again, discussion among likeminded people amplified the members' pre-discussion tendencies.

A similar experiment involved adults who, on the basis of an initial screening, were classified into gender-mixed groups according to their views concerning the social roles of women. Once sorted into "feminist" and "chauvinist" groups, each discussed among themselves the merits of various statements about the role of women in society – statements like "a woman should be as free as a man to propose marriage," and "women with children should not work outside the home if they don't have to financially." The result was that members of the feminist discussion group became more pro-feminist – and vice versa.

In 2005, a collection of Coloradoans were sorted according to an initial screening test into "liberal" and "conservative" groups. Each group was then asked to discuss the following three policy issues that admitted of an obvious liberal-conservative divide: same-sex marriage, affirmative action, and international treaties to combat global warming. The pattern of belief polarization was observed. After discussion within likeminded groups, liberal participants, who were antecedently disposed to favor a global warming treaty, came to endorse more enthusiastically the proposition that the United States should enter into such a treaty. Conservatives who were initially neutral on the idea of such a treaty came to ardently oppose it after discussion with fellow conservatives. Similarly, attitudes towards same-sex civil unions and affirmative action belief-polarized following group discussion: liberal support intensified, while opposition among conservatives grew more resolute.

It is important to note that belief polarization renders us more extreme in two distinct senses of that term. First, when we surround ourselves only with likeminded others, we become inordinately *confident* in our commitments. Thus, in the course of belief polarization, one who is inclined to believe that climate change is a hoax will become more *convinced* that it is. This means that she will come to hold her antecedent belief with a degree of confidence that is further out of step with her evidence than before. Second, belief polarization also leads us to adopt *more extreme beliefs*. For example, in experiments with juries, when jurors are all agreed that a punitive award is in order, in the course of their discussion each member comes to favor a more severe punishment. In short, when people get together with likeminded others, each intensifies their level of confidence in a belief that is more extreme than the belief with which they started.

Part of what makes belief polarization so disconcerting is its ubiquity. It has been extensively studied for more than 50 years, and found to be operative within groups of all kinds, formal and informal. Furthermore, belief polarization does not discriminate between different kinds of belief. Likeminded groups polarize regardless of whether they are discussing banal matters of fact, matters of personal taste, or questions about value. What's more, the phenomenon operates regardless of the explicit point of the group's discussion. Likeminded groups polarize when they are trying to decide an action that the group will take, and they polarize also when there is no specific decision to be reached. Finally, the phenomenon is prevalent regardless of group members' nationality, race, gender, religion, economic status, and level of education. Rarely is a social-psychological finding so robust.[1]

---

1 Interested readers may consult the Appendix in Cass Sunstein's *Going to Extremes: How Like Minds Unite and Divide* (New York: Oxford University Press, 2009) for a review of the research.

How Does Belief Polarization Work?

Our widespread susceptibility to belief polarization raises the question of how it works. Two views suggest themselves: the *informational* account and the *comparison* account. On the first, discussion with likeminded others exposes us to a high concentration of affirming reasons and ideas. Moreover, in such contexts, there is typically a scarcity of countervailing or disconfirming considerations. Consequently, group members absorb the new information, and revise their own view in light of it. As the new information confirms their antecedent view, they become more extreme advocates.

Although the informational account surely captures part of what drives belief polarization, it cannot be the entire story. For one thing, belief polarization has been found to occur in groups even when new and novel information is not presented. In fact, it has been found to occur even in contexts where group interactions involve no exchange of information at all beyond simply agreeing on an issue.

This suggests an alternative, the *comparison* view, which holds that belief polarization results from in-group comparisons. Group members care about how they are perceived by the other members. In the course of discussion, they get a better feel for the general tendencies within the group, and, wanting to appear to others neither as a half-hearted outlier nor as an over-the-top fanatic, they update their opinions so that their view lies notably above what they perceive to be the mean, but beneath what they regard as unacceptably hardline. Now, given that group members are engaging simultaneously in this kind of recalibration, the tendency to escalating extremity is to be expected.

Although more promising than the strictly informational view, the comparison account is still lacking. Just as belief polarization can

occur in the absence of the exchange of supporting reasons or information, it can be induced in the absence of in-group comparisons,
too. Indeed, the phenomenon can be activated even in the absence
of anything that would count as *interaction* among the members of
the likeminded group. It is not real time *comparisons* that drive the
phenomenon so much as the subject's own internal estimations of
the dominant tendencies within his or her identity group. So neither
information-exchange nor in-group comparison is strictly necessary
for the effect; rather, the relevant shifts occur simply in light of group-
affiliated *corroboration* of one's views. That is, belief polarization
can occur simply when an individual is caused to feel that a group
with which she identifies widely shares a view that she espouses. She
need not hear any reasons in favor of the view, nor need she be in the
presence of other members of the group with whom she can compare
herself. Instead, the realization that one's belief is popular among
one's identity group suffices for belief polarization.

Thus a third account, the *corroboration* view, holds that shifts
towards extremity can occur simply as a result of in-group corroboration. Corroboration from our peers makes us feel *good* about our
shared beliefs, and this makes us feel *affirmed* in our social identity.
In turn, when we feel affirmed in this way, we shift toward extremity.

So it turns out that although belief polarization predictably occurs
in *discussion* among likeminded people, this is not necessary for the
effect. Indeed, corroboration can come by way of highly indirect
channels. For example, presenting a subject who identifies as liberal
with a chart showing that liberals widely oppose genetically modified
food can prompt belief polarization. And exposure to a poll showing
that conservatives overwhelmingly favor a particular military action
can produce an extremity shift in the belief content of a conservative
already favorably disposed to that action.

An intriguing implication follows. The social environment itself can trigger extremity shifts. These prompts need not be verbal, explicit, or literal; they can be merely implicit signals to group members that some belief is prevalent among them – hats, pins, campaign signs, logos, and gestures are all potential initiators of belief polarization. Further, as corroboration is really a matter of numbers, those with the power to present the *appearance* of widespread acceptance among a particular group of some idea thereby have the power to induce extremity shifts among those who identify with that group.

It is sometimes claimed that the proper response to belief polarization is to diversify our sources of information. This is of course a good idea in any case. However, the corroboration view of belief polarization suggests that this measure is insufficient. Irrespective of the choices we make to expand our informational exposure, the physical and social surroundings that we inhabit in our day-to-day life can transform us into more extreme versions of ourselves.

The Polarization Dynamic

In order to understand the problem that polarization poses for democratic politics, we need to understand the way in which political polarization and belief polarization are linked.

Begin by noticing that political polarization is not a new phenomenon. Political intransigence, deadlock, and resentment are familiar features of the political order. And, arguably, certain forms of interpartisan conflict are democratically healthy. Observe also that belief polarization need not be obviously politically problematic. The phenomenon entails that we are less in control of our beliefs and related attitudes than we would like. This might be bad news for us as cognitive creatures, but it is not clearly troubling for us in our roles as citizens. After all, moving toward more extreme versions of our political beliefs might, in the end, place us closer to the truth. So, at least from this perspective, is polarization maybe not really a problem after all?

Yes and no. One feature of belief polarization that is not frequently commented on is that, as we become more extreme versions of ourselves, our beliefs about those with whom we disagree also shift. Again, repeated interactions with our fellow partisans transform us into more extreme advocates of our partisan views, but in addition make nonpartisans look more alien to us. As we belief-polarize, we begin to regard those with whom we disagree as increasingly inscrutable, irrational, ignorant, and unreliable. We also lose the capacity to recognize nuance in their views and reasons; that is, belief polarization leads us to regard our opponents' views as monolithic, brute, and extreme. Moreover, we come to regard larger and larger portions of their behavior as explicable simply by their political commitments; in other words, as belief polarization takes effect, we come to see more and more of what our opponents do – their shopping habits, what they eat, their profession, where they live, how they spend their weekends – as expressing their misguided political beliefs.

In this connection, notice how much of popular political discourse aims at disparaging the other side's *lifestyle* and *consumer* choices. Once we are belief-polarized, a Starbucks coffee or a pickup truck are not *simply* a drink and an automobile. They're *expressions* of their owners' political identities and allegiances. Thus, in attacking the other side's preference for fancy coffee, we take ourselves to be assailing their political views. And the tight correlation between political allegiances and consumer preferences has not been lost on commercial firms. One has only to observe the difference between the interior design of a Starbucks and that of a Dunkin' Donuts to see that the two companies see themselves as serving drastically different political demographics. One drinks coffee in order to pretend to be in a café in a foreign country; the other seeks fuel in order to make it through the workday.

The other-regarding dimension of the belief polarization phenomenon provides the connection between belief and political polarization. As belief polarization leads us to regard our political rivals as increasingly benighted, irrational, and unreasonable, we become more and more inclined to distrust, dislike, and resent those whom we regard as our opponents. We thus become ever more involved only with our political allies, and this in turn contributes further to belief polarization. Our political alliances thereby become more tightly knit and exclusionary. Consequently, political parties and their leaders are incentivized to punctuate (and overstate) their policy and platform differences. All this occurs within a self-perpetuating, spiraling dynamic that intensifies civic divisions and interpartisan animosity. That is, belief polarization sets in motion a broader dynamic that not only codifies political polarization, but also erodes our capacity for civil political disagreement, and thus democracy.

Polarization Undermines Democracy

It is worth emphasizing that the dynamic of both belief and political polarization results not only in a condition where political opponents cannot productively disagree with one another; it also creates social conditions where we become increasingly disinclined to regard those who are unlike ourselves as our political equals. Accordingly, the polarization dynamic prompts us to regard political dissensus as itself conclusive evidence of the political incompetence of our opponents, and thus a failure of proper democracy. This is obviously a perversion of democracy; as was argued earlier, democracy is a political system devoted to the idea that equal citizens are bound to disagree about politics. Once we regard those who disagree with us politically as *ipso facto* unfit for democratic citizenship, we lose sight of the basis upon which they are nonetheless our equals. What's more, we tacitly come to embrace a conception of democracy according to which a person must agree with our own views in order to be our political equal and capable of citizenship. Democracy without disagreement! That's no democracy at all.

But that's pretty much where we find ourselves. Our democracy is devolving into a brawl among political factions that can no longer discern a basis for the political equality of their opponents. The result is a politics driven by the aspiration to humiliate and denigrate those with whom one disagrees in the hope that, once adequately dispirited, they will quietly disengage and simply submit to the power of one's own faction. Democracy is thereby transmogrified into a cold civil war. The trouble is that once we acknowledge that we are now engaged in a cold civil war rather than in a program of collective self-government among equals, we must also jettison the idea that political power is being exercised legitimately. Hence, there is nothing to prevent our cold civil war from erupting into a hot one.

Consider a curious phenomenon particularly prevalent among professed conservatives – that of reveling in "liberal tears." We have the "coal rolling" phenomenon – that of converting one's pickup truck so that it can release black exhaust into the windshields of Priuses. There is the fact that James Delingpole of *Breitbart* wrote a book titled *365 Ways to Drive a Liberal Crazy*. Or the simple animus of a bumper sticker with the invocation of Trump's re-election being something to cheer for, if only for the sake of causing pain to progressives: "TRUMP 2020 – Make Liberals Cry Again." It seems the height of civic vice to adopt a political stance strictly for the sake of expressing one's contempt of another group. But this is the contempt that the polarization dynamic breeds. Perhaps a cold civil war is the best we can hope for, but it's a condition that falls far short of the democratic ideal.

5

Political Ignorance

One of the most common frustrations with democracy is the political ignorance of the rank-and-file democratic citizen. Citizens in the United States generally cannot explain the fundamental workings of the US Constitution, do not know the requirements for holding the office of president, and cannot recite the freedoms guaranteed in the First Amendment. Polling research routinely reveals stunningly high levels of ignorance regarding even the most basic facts about our government: citizens generally cannot distinguish the branches of government and cannot describe the division of power among them. Many of us would be unable to pass a grade school civics test. The phenomenon isn't confined to the United States, either. For example, in the months leading up to the monumental Brexit referendum in 2016, research showed that British citizens were largely ignorant of relevant facts, including the size of the non-British population living in the UK and the degree to which EU countries invest in the UK. And a 2008 study showed that 75 percent of Canadian citizens could not correctly identify their head of state. The political ignorance of democratic citizens is nearly boundless.

Public ignorance is disconcerting. But it also poses a serious challenge to democracy. We have already said that democracy is a system of collective self-government among political equals who disagree about political matters, and we have noted that political argument thus lies at the core of the democratic ideal. As we have also emphasized, political disagreement in a democracy is always disagreement among political equals; thus, citizens are required to conduct themselves civilly in political argument. Civil conduct amidst political disagreement expresses our commitment to one another's political equality. However, the staggering levels of political ignorance that prevail in contemporary democracies challenge that commitment. Ever since Plato, the widespread ignorance of the citizens has functioned as a central argument against democracy. And so we must ask: why should equal political power be apportioned to citizens who are so ignorant? Or, to formulate the same thought in a different way, why must *you* regard those whom you believe to be fundamentally mistaken about the most important political issues as your political equals? Shouldn't their incompetence disqualify them for democratic citizenship? If you've ever felt umbrage at the fact that your neighbor or relative who is so deeply misinformed about matters that there seems no point in talking to them nevertheless gets to vote and thereby cancel out the force of your vote, then you've felt the pull of this problem.

Given the overall view we have proposed of democracy, the challenge of public ignorance is especially formidable. In fact, many democratic theorists take the phenomenon of public ignorance to show that our basic ideal of democracy as a system by which political equals can enact collective self-rule by means of proper argumentation is irrevocably flawed. Of these, many claim that the extent of public ignorance found among democratic citizens shows that democracy is rather simply a mechanism for the popular selection of government office holders. We can call this alternative view of democracy *minimalism*. Minimalists hold that the lofty ideals of truth-seeking by means of civil political disagreement among political equals should be jettisoned from our understanding of democracy. So, if we are to make a plausible case for civil political disagreement, perhaps we need first to show why we think that widespread and deep public ignorance of political basics doesn't entail a minimalist view of democracy.

Ways of Being Ignorant

In case it's not already clear, we begin by explicitly conceding that the empirical work on public ignorance is extensive and uncommonly univocal. Democratic citizens are indeed stunningly ignorant of the basics of the political order in which they participate. We do not contest this.

However, those who employ the findings regarding public ignorance as an argument for minimalism frequently take the public ignorance data to speak for themselves. They *report* the findings of widespread public ignorance, and then proceed as if the dismal portrait of the democratic citizen simply entails a minimalist conception of democracy. Things are not so simple as that. In order to figure out what prescription to draw from the ignorance data, we need to do some philosophical thinking about what the data mean. And here puzzles emerge.

As the concept is employed in this literature, *ignorance* is most frequently taken simply to be a matter of false believing. Accordingly, citizens who believe that the president directly controls gas prices are claimed to be ignorant. But so too are citizens who can't name all three branches of government, as are those who can't name their state senators. However, even though these are arguably all cases appropriately characterized as ignorance, the three cases above actually present different ways of being ignorant. In the first, the subjects have a false belief; in the second, the subjects lack knowledge about the structure of the federal government established in the US Constitution; in the third, the subjects are uninformed about who occupies a particular office.

To be sure, these are all cases in which citizens are falling short. But as the failing is different in each case, so too should the remedy vary. We suspect that many citizens who can't name the three branches require only a reminder; those who don't know who their senators are can simply be told their names; and those who think that the president controls gas prices need to be instructed about the powers of the president (they may also need a lesson in basic economics).

We take it that this is simple enough to be uncontroversial. However, once we expand the inventory of cases to include a broader range of phenomena properly referred to as "ignorance," we find ourselves reaching for distinctions and ideas that are largely absent from the empirical work. For example, there is a fundamental difference between true belief, false belief, and justified belief. A belief is true or false depending on the way the world is; but a belief is justified or not depending on the nature and extent of the evidence available to the believer. Accordingly, not every false belief is held without justification. One's best evidence can lead one to a false belief. And some true beliefs are unjustified, as in the case of a lucky guess.

With this initial distinction adopted, others quickly follow. For one thing, there is a difference between a belief's being justified *subjectively* (justified *given the evidence the person has*) and *objectively* (justified *given all the evidence there is*). There is then a nearby distinction between a person *forming the wrong belief* given her evidence, her *failing to form a belief at all* when her evidence warrants belief-formation, and *forming a belief* based on insufficient evidence. There is also a related distinction between two foci in evaluating belief: the person ("believer evaluation") and the person's belief ("belief evaluation"). This in turn supports another distinction between cases of unjustified belief for which the person is blameworthy, and those in which blame is not appropriate. Finally, there is a distinction between evaluations of *how a person acquires* beliefs, how she *revises* beliefs, and how she *sustains* belief in the face of apparently countervailing evidence.

The area of philosophy that explores these matters is called *epistemology* (Greek for *theory of knowledge*). And the foregoing is the stuff of Epistemology 101. Yet this very rough menu of elementary concepts enables us to introduce some of the necessary nuance into the conception of public ignorance. Take the false proposition that the president directly controls the price of gasoline. Now let's distinguish a few cases in which a subject has the false belief that *the president directly controls the price of gasoline.*

1   Ann believes that the president directly controls the price of gasoline because the otherwise credible news channel she regularly watches constantly features reports that blame the president for the price of gas.

2   Bruce believes that the president directly controls the price of gasoline despite being regularly exposed to sources of correction and evidence sufficient to require him to revise his belief.

3   Carol believes that the president directly controls the price of gasoline, dislikes the president intensely, and is disposed to blame him for anything that seems bad to her.

4   Dennis believes that the president directly controls the price of gasoline on the basis of an elaborate conspiracy theory according to which the president is secretly a member of the Saudi royal

family, and is able to control gasoline prices in virtue of that familial tie.

All four cases would register as instances of ignorance in the relevant studies. Nevertheless, *ignorance* is not univocal across the cases; that is, Ann, Bruce, Carol, and Dennis are in strikingly different conditions. They are all ignorant, for sure, but their ignorance takes different forms, and so will need different remedies. Ann is not obviously blameworthy for her false belief, and she might be subjectively justified in believing as she does. After all, her false belief accords with the evidence she has access to, and she has adequate reason to take her source of evidence to be reliable; it's just that her news source has *failed* her. Bruce is irresponsible in his belief and likely blameworthy for failing to adequately respond to the evidence he has. But note that Bruce might be criticizable on these grounds even in cases where he has true beliefs. He might have a *habit* of not responding properly to his evidence, in which case his problem is not the falsity of his false beliefs, but the irresponsible processes he uses in forming his beliefs. One is tempted to say that Carol is worse than Bruce in this regard. She is *reckless* in the way she forms her beliefs, believing anything that fits her negative disposition towards the president. So, like Bruce, she is criticizable even in cases where she holds a *true* belief about the president's culpability for some politically bad action. And Dennis's case cannot be assessed given the information we have. The conspiracy theory underwriting his belief that the president directly controls the price of gasoline might be the product of a third party's manipulation of the information to which he is exposed, and this information could provide what Dennis reasonably (but falsely) regards as evidence for his belief. Moreover, Dennis might not be mistaken about the power of the president *in his role as president*; recall that he believes the president (*the particular person and not merely the person who happens to occupy the office,* one might add) controls the prices in his role as secret member of Saudi royalty. Anyway, Dennis might be utterly blameless, despite being the worst-off in the group.

Let's bring this back around to the public ignorance findings we mentioned in the previous section. Imagine that Elizabeth incorrectly responds to a survey question about the three branches of government established in the US Constitution. She might be ignorant in the same way that Ann is ignorant. Elizabeth might have false beliefs about the three branches because she has had the misfortune of being exposed to misleading information from what would otherwise reasonably be considered a reliable source of such information. Alternatively, she might be in a condition more like Bruce's. She might hold false beliefs about the three branches *despite* having accessed all the necessary evidence for forming true beliefs. The data gleaned from the political ignorance literature does not distinguish between these two different ways in which Elizabeth might be ignorant regarding the three branches of government established by the US Constitution. What's more, consider Fred, who correctly answers the survey questions, but only because he's a lucky guesser. Fred would register as *not ignorant*! Similar points can be made about the findings concerning public ignorance leading up to the Brexit referendum. Arguably, a lot of the false beliefs among UK citizens surrounding Brexit was the product of misleading information rather than inattention or recklessness on the part of the citizens. Had some of them been exposed to different, more accurate, information, their beliefs would have been different. Again, the data do not incorporate the necessary distinctions; thus, it is not clear what conclusion to draw from the findings.

Our broader point is that the public ignorance literature doesn't employ the conceptual apparatus required for adequately under-standing exactly what the problem of public ignorance is. We know that, given the kind of power it collectively wields, the citizenry falls far short of any reasonable threshold of political understanding. But we don't know whether public ignorance is a problem of widespread false and unfounded beliefs, widespread false but founded beliefs, irresponsible or reckless belief forming processes, or (as is likely) varied combinations of them all. In short, we can't tell from the data whether citizens are politically ignorant *despite* having adequate access to everything they would need to form correct beliefs, or not. Alas, it would be difficult to design a large-scale research program that could detect the relevant nuances, so it is not at all clear what follows for democracy.

Tribal Citizens

But doesn't this result play into the minimalists' hands? They might say that *whatever* ignorance amounts to, it's incontrovertible that ignorance prevails among the citizenry to a staggering and unaccep-table degree. So much the *worse* for democracy!

However, note that it matters for democracy whether the prevailing kind of ignorance tends to be the kind afflicting Ann rather than Bruce. After all, Ann is doing her job as a democratic citizen; in her case the problem lies with the public institutions tasked with informing the public. Until we can discern in the political ignorance data the relevant differences between Ann and Bruce, it's simply not clear whether the data recommend minimalism over our argumen-tation-based view of democracy.

Yet there's a different kind of concern that emerges from the public ignorance literature. What one finds there is a pretty stable breakdown within the democratic citizenry between a large segment of tribal citizens who are highly politically active and opinionated and who also *take themselves* to be exceedingly politically well informed, but in fact are highly ignorant, and a much smaller segment that is far less active politically but reasonably well informed. In between these two groups is an intermediate-sized segment that is uninterested in politics and so is largely politically inactive. The problem is that democracy encourages us to be politically active and highly opinionated, regardless of whether or not we are in fact well informed. And so the vast majority of democratic citizens are devoted loyalists to one political tribe or another, while also being ignorant of the very thing they claim to be expert about. As the tribal segment of the populace far outnumbers the segment that is well informed, democracy devolves into a power struggle among the ignorant tribes. This is obviously a far cry from our conception of democracy as collective self-rule among civilly disagreeing political equals.

Let's concede this depiction of the *personae* of democracy. What follows? Some have suggested that the upshot is that democracy should be replaced with some form of rule-by-experts. Others propose that democracy should be *tempered* by some arrangement according to which people would be apportioned political power according to their level of political knowledge, with the more ignorant getting proportionately less power than the more knowledgeable. We cannot evaluate these ideas here. The thing to remember, though, is that these alternative proposals must be evaluated *comparatively* – that is, we must weigh them according to how they are likely to function against existing democratic arrangements. Here, we think that our version of democracy prevails.

Here's why. Recall that the tribal segment of the democratic population also is most likely to *regard itself* as the most informed and knowledgeable. They are the loudest and the most ignorant, but they also regard themselves as the best suited for citizenship. That is, unlike the class of knowledgeable but less active citizens, they cannot *embrace* an accurate description of themselves. It is, after all, part of the nature of their tribalism to see themselves as the politically smartest guys in every room. From the *inside*, their tribal biases look like principles, their vices look like virtues, and their tribal allegiances look like perfectly rational commitments to Justice, Freedom, and Equality. And this is as it should be. To sincerely assess one's reasoning as plagued by bias is to lose confidence in one's reasoning and its products. To assess one's belief as the product of systematic dysfunction is to see the belief itself as corrupt. To regard one's political allegiances as driven strictly by tribal psychological forces is to see them as degraded. In other words, delusion and self-ignorance (perhaps self-deception, too) are ineradicable parts of the political profile of the tribal citizen. Consequently, the tribalists *must* regard themselves as belonging to the tiny class of highly informed citizens. That's how tribal epistemology works.

Consequently, the call for some kind of departure from the democratic norm of affording to all citizens an equal say will strike the tribal citizens as especially attractive. After all, they take themselves to be the politically most knowledgeable citizens, and the ones most interested in politics. So they will expect any proposal to apportion power according to knowledge to deliver to them more political power. What's more, as they will see members of opposing tribes as especially incompetent and incapable, they will expect any proper allocation of political power to give themselves *decisively* more power than their political opposition. In short, each tribal citizen will see himself as exceedingly well qualified for a kingly share of power, and will simultaneously regard members of opposing political tribes as deserving of minimal political say, if not complete disenfranchisement.

Consider what follows. Any proposal for expert rule that does not place the tribal citizen in a position of great power will be received by him as yet another political corruption, a power grab by their political inferiors and enemies. However, under any arrangement by which political power is apportioned according to political knowledge, there will need to be *some* determination of who the real knowers are and what the reliable markers of the relevant kinds of knowledge will be. Who will make the relevant determinations? Moreover, given what the tribal segment of the population is like, there simply will be no way of instituting such a strategy without thereby inflaming tribal hostilities among political opponents. All tribalists will see themselves and their allies as uniquely fit to rule. But, in fact, no tribalist would rise to the top of any scheme in which political power is distributed according to political knowledge. The result is an all-out power struggle among tribalists. So how, exactly, could this be better than democracy?

To be clear, these arguments provide no solution to the problem that public ignorance poses for our conception of democracy-as-public argument. No surprise there. There *is no democratic solution* to the problem of public ignorance. What our argument has shown is that, since it's not clear exactly what public ignorance *is*, it's not clear what its implications are with respect to democracy. Still, it is clear that once we find out more precisely what public ignorance is, we will be in a better position to think about how best to address it. However, it strikes us that in order to figure out what public ignorance is, we need to sustain our commitments to democracy understood as collective self-government by means of civil political disagreement among political equals. Only under those conditions can we regard public ignorance as a problem to be addressed.

6

Simulated Argument

Civil political disagreement is something we all value, but it is not easy to achieve. Perhaps this is why civil political disagreement is so often mimicked, counterfeited. In the heat of an agitated political debate, we like to regard ourselves as the reasonable party. But if we're being honest with ourselves, we all know how difficult it is to argue well about politics. One way to improve is to try to think more clearly about how arguments work. Several distinct challenges surround the endeavor. Perhaps the most obvious of these is that reasoning is, well, demanding. Further, because of the demandingness of reasoning, humans are prone to certain errors – these are called *fallacies* – and this tendency can confound our sincerest efforts to argue well. Add to this that civil disagreement is *risky*. In the course of a proper argument, one exposes oneself to scrutiny, and this means that one might have to revise or relinquish one's commitments. These two challenges are related. We're prone to commit fallacies partly because we tend to be averse to changing our beliefs.

Unsurprisingly, there is a vast "critical thinking" industry devoted to producing textbooks that train students to detect and avoid fallacies. To be clear, this is an important aspect of arguing well. However, it is not the whole story. Although we will discuss certain fallacies in this chapter, our central aim is to highlight a different kind of challenge to proper argument. When called upon to deal with others who disagree with us, we are prone to adopt approaches that can undermine civil political disagreement by rendering our engagements merely *proxies* for argument, or *simulations*. In such cases, one might conform to the external requirements of proper argumentation – indeed, one might even be "civil" in the popular sense of being calm, soft-spoken, and courteous. But in the cases we have in mind, it's all a charade.

We emphasized earlier that it is part of our civic duty to argue well. When engaging in argument, citizens must conduct themselves in ways that help to achieve a better understanding of the matter in dispute. It is by means of such conduct that we acknowledge the political equality of our fellow citizens, despite ongoing disagreement. However, when one is in the thick of a dispute, it's easy to conduct oneself in a way that undercuts the civic role of argumentation, distorting it into an expression of disrespect and even contempt for those with whom we disagree.

So let's go back to square one and consider two different ways in which we can fail at argument, despite attempting to argue. The first consists in thinking about argument strictly as the means to winning converts. Call this the *rhetorical view* of argument. It holds that, as the only purpose of argument is to convince others, securing agreement is the *criterion* for successful argument. Yet it turns out that although we often engage in argument with the aim of convincing others, this cannot be the *standard* for proper argument. When we argue strictly in order to win converts, we fail to argue at all.

The second consists in taking argument to have as its aim *solidifying* agreement among one's allies. When disagreement is approached in this way, one treats one's interlocutors as mere props. Frequently, this leads one to misrepresent the opposition's views. Engaging with opportunistic distortions of one's interlocutors makes no contribution to civil disagreement. Although, when engaged in argument, we frequently take ourselves in part to be speaking for those who are on our side of the issue, when we see fomenting in-group solidarity as the point of dispute, we fail at argument. Think of every time you've watched a political discussion unfold but both sides are more interested in reiterating the things that those who already agree with them would say – they don't try to address those with whom they disagree, but they address only those already convinced. That *looks like* they are arguing, but they are really only putting on a charade of argumentative exchange. Instead, the whole time, they are really addressing different audiences simply with the objective of solidifying their adherence. It's all a series of misses.

These two strategies for merely simulating argument are pervasive in contemporary political discourse. As we will show in the closing section of this chapter, they have a particular culmination in the culture of political memes. Among members of the alt-right, the memes of Pepe the Frog, NPC's, and the Honkler show how deeply the divides run between the sides, where the best case one can make against the other side is to simply express contempt for it.

Argument as Rhetoric

Disagreement can be frustrating. It gets in the way of plans and obstructs collective action. Moreover, disagreement involves the attempt to *correct* others, which can escalate hostility. In political contexts, these frustrations are intensified, because how we will live together is on the line. Argument is about resolving disagreement – it's about trying to solve problems and bring others around to believing what's true.

It is tempting to associate proper argument with the "art of rhetoric," the skill of bringing others in line with one's own opinions. It should be mentioned that this art is not as baldly manipulative as it might appear, for the aim is not simply to *quash* disagreement, but to *actually convince* others. Thus, artful rhetoricians take careful account of the views of their audience; they attempt not only to reason *with* the audience, but to reason *from* the audience's perspectives to the rhetorician's preferred conclusion. Sounds good, right?

Indeed. This rhetorical view of argument appears to appreciate the fact that in argument one is confronting *another reasoning creature*, a mind with ideas of its own. It therefore counsels arguers to seek to begin from the other's point of view, and consequently calls arguers to actually speak to each other by addressing each other's reasons, such as they may be. This encourages arguers to place themselves in the position of the interlocutor. This is all commendable, and notice how it seems very close to the notion of civility in political disagreement that we've been developing.

However, the rhetorical view is fixated strictly on moving others. Argumentation, then, begins only once we have settled on a view, and seek to promulgate it. Argumentation thus is not a process by which we turn a critical eye inward and attempt to rationally assess our own views. Nor is it a process by which we attempt to figure things out, or discern what views to adopt in the first place. In short, the rhetorical view sees argument as essentially other-directed, in the service of disseminating one's already settled view.

So the rhetorical view offers a risk-free approach to argument. As the entire point of argument is to convince others, in engaging in argument, one never truly exposes oneself to the rational scrutiny of one's critics. Thus one's own ideas are never really put on the line. This renders the apparent civility of the rhetorical view as a kind of sham. One insists that others engage in critical thinking simply so that they might come to hold one's own view, but one is never required to field objections. This is counterfeit civility.

To appreciate this charge against the rhetorical view, contrast it with an alternative, *epistemic* view. This view holds that we argue in order to find out what's best supported by the evidence and reasons. It is by argumentative exchange that we come to see more fully what reasons and evidence there are, and thus come to occupy a better vantage point from which to evaluate our options, including the beliefs we already hold. In this way, the epistemic view sees argument as a *critical* activity aimed at the evaluation of views. But note that argument then is also a *self-critical* process by which we can assess our own views.

The epistemic view locates civility in seeing others as partners in the common pursuit of believing what's right by believing what the best available reasons and evidence favor. By contrast, the rhetorical view has it that I engage civilly with you when I take you as you are – with the beliefs you already have – and attempt to rationally move you from your current position toward mine. The epistemic view holds that I civilly engage with you when I regard you as a partner in a search for truth, and thus a fellow source of reasons, ideas, evidence, and objections.

From this contrast, others come into view. First, the rhetorical view holds that there could be no argumentative success that is not also a shift toward greater consensus. The epistemic view rejects this; it holds that the success of an argument has to do with the relation between the conclusion and the relevant reasons. A good argument might not convince one's audience; indeed, a good argument could result in there being greater disagreement. Think, for example, of any time you and someone you know exchanged reasons, nobody changed their minds, but you understood each other and your respective views better. You may have consequently opposed each other more stringently, but you also did so more informedly. That's progress, right? Not according to the rhetorical view. But it is progress on the epistemic view. That's a pretty significant difference.

Second, the rhetorical view sees argument as a one-way street. Pushback from the audience functions on this view only as feedback about how the rhetorician should proceed; there is nothing in argumentation that could *require* a rhetorical arguer to relinquish or revise her view. By contrast, the epistemic view is dialogical. It sees argument as the give-and-take of reasons, and it understands that in this process, both arguers and their audiences could discover new reasons to modify their views. That is, pushback from the audience can constitute a *refutation* of the epistemic arguer's view. In this way, on the epistemic view, argumentation is a collective intellectual risk. In undertaking to convince you of one of my beliefs, I expose myself to your rational scrutiny and thus recognize the possibility that my beliefs might be incorrect.

Consider a final critical difference between these two views of argument. Imagine a rhetorician having made an argument in support of the rhetorical theory of argument, with the result of having failed to convince her audience. This renders the rhetorician's argument a failure. Yet the rhetorician cannot see this failure as a reason to rethink her view of argument. After all, she holds that argument is exclusively directed toward winning new converts to her views. That she has failed to convince her audience of the rhetorical view poses no challenge to it; it merely shows that she had employed the wrong rhetorical tools for gaining their assent. This is because the rhetorical view values only conviction, not truth, cogency, or rationality – the things the epistemic view prizes.

In political disagreement, we engage in argument in order to convince others of our view. That's as it should be. But when argument is seen *simply* as a tool for winning agreement, it turns pathological. It loses its self-critical function, and thus manifests what might be thought of as a *patient* model of disagreement: *they* need to be convinced to adopt our view, *we* need to convince them. But civil disagreement calls for a *partner* model: we must see those with whom we disagree as fellow arguers, participants who are capable of responding critically to what we say. In order to be civil, we must embrace our vulnerability to the rational scrutiny of our opposition. This is partly how earnest and heated disputation can be an expression of our commitment to one another's equality. Without this component, there really is no argument, but mere proselytizing.

Argument as Group Affirmation

There is often more at stake in argument than our favored answer to the question under discussion. The beliefs we hold form a web, and so revising one belief often causes us to revise others. Additionally, our views are never strictly our *own*. Our beliefs locate us within social categories, and we often *identify* with these groupings. Observe the frequency with which people say things like "As a Christian, I believe … " and "Given my liberal sensibilities, I think … ." When it comes to the views that really matter to us, we often see our beliefs as expressing group membership. Moreover, we take our steadfastness in those beliefs as indicative of our authenticity. It's not too far of a stretch to say that, in some argumentative contexts, our very identities are on the line. Consequently, we argue sometimes as a way of *affirming* our group identity.

This feature of argumentation gives rise to a second kind of simulated argument. Sometimes, one sees argumentative exchange as not having to do with winning converts, but rather with enforcing group cohesion. The worlds of political commentary that one finds online and on cable news are rich with examples: in presenting arguments against the other side, the commentator is really enforcing a party line, putting the home team's talking points on display so that fellow partisans can recite them. When argument is mimicked in this way, one isn't really *arguing with* one's interlocutor at all. Rather, one uses the interlocutor simply as a piece of scenery against which to perform for an audience of one's allies in a way that affirms a shared identity. This is argument as strictly spectacle, designed to circle-the-wagons rather than deepen understanding.

Of course, as it is a mode of simulated *argument,* those who take this approach nonetheless must handle the interlocutor. Although he is essentially a prop, the interlocutor cannot fade into the background, but must be placed at center stage. The trick is to give the opponent the spotlight without really giving him any substantive lines. He must appear only as the foil, something dull but nonetheless obstructing that the star of the show can valiantly overcome, "shut down," and "own."

We take it that the strategy is familiar. In fact, there is a well-established name for one version of the tactic. One commits the *straw man fallacy* when one distorts an interlocutor's view in a way that makes it more easily criticized. In effect, one replaces an actual opponent with one made of straw – a set-piece that is easily knocked over and cannot fight back. When it is deployed successfully, those who are already on the side of the person erecting the straw man are made to feel as if their view has prevailed in argument.

For example, consider the following from a campus newspaper: "Students have requested that there be a pub on the college campus for informal gatherings and receptions. The administration opposes the pub because they 'refuse to subsidize student bacchanalia.'" The problem here is that the request for a pub, even from college students, is not a call for wild, destructive binges. The administration has constructed a straw man of the students' request. Accordingly, what is presented as the reason for the administration's opposition is no reason at all. What's more, the straw man draws upon a perception, common among those who identify with the administration, that students are irresponsible and cannot be trusted to behave like adults. In this way, the straw man is not only a failure to engage, it serves to *end* discussion of a campus pub by solidifying among those who identify with the administration an unflattering view of the students.

The straw man takes a variety of forms. These range from the standard version captured in the case above, to the variant known as the *weak man fallacy*. Here, one chooses to engage only with those opponents who have markedly weak arguments; one engages in argument with the weak man and prevails, but then presents the exchange to a sympathetic audience as if one had argued with the *very best* of the opposition. Although the weak man involves an honest engagement with one's interlocutor, it nonetheless manifests a failure of argumentation, as it also uses the interlocutor in staging a performance for an audience of one's allies. They want to see the opposition overcome in argument; the weak man is sure to give the people what they want.

A third variant is perpetrated when one creates a pastiche of distortions of one's dialectical opponent – it is not composed simply of a single distortion, but rather a slew of mischaracterizations bent on representing one's opponents in the worst light. Call this the *burning man*. In deploying the burning man fallacy, one not only stuffs an opposing figure with straw, but then proceeds to surround it with more tinder and additional flammable material, with the intention of committing the view at issue to the flames, along with whole traditions, movements, and ways of thinking.

The burning man is common when specific disagreements reflect larger divides. And once a disagreement at hand is seen as a manifestation of the larger divide, all the bad images of the side that one abhors now accumulate around one's dialectical opponent. It happens quickly, and it yields little more than revulsion with those on the other side.

Sean Hannity of Fox News is a master of the burning man. He presented in one short segment a characterization of the "crop of 2020 Democratic hopefuls" as:

pushing to give 16-year-olds the right to vote, even though you can't drink until you're 21. They're promising to stack the Supreme Court so they get enough justices that think their way and will legislate from the bench. And they're proposing an end to the Electoral College … Government-run health care and complete takeover of the health care industry – yes, run by the state … And government-run education – now they're going to add pre-K and college education. They haven't done a better enough job with kindergarten through 12th grade? And they will have government consolidation of all guns and gun laws and government-run clean energy through the government takeover of the energy sector … Government-run universal income, government-paid-for vacation, government-sponsored healthy food … [T]hey will tell you how to run your business.

There will be government promises for everything and for everybody – you'll never have a worry in the world. But you also will give up all of your freedom.

The strategy here is to collect a set of views – specifically those objectionable to his target audience of conservatives – and pile them together into a heap of disagreeable ideas. His strategy is to show not just that any one of the commitments is wrong, but that they come as a wholesale package of something not to be argued against, but simply reviled. He concludes:

Democrats don't share the values of our framers. They want power for themselves, and they want it at all cost … It is a blatant, dramatic, frightening attempt to alter America in ways that will make it unrecognizable and forever destroy the greatest economic wealth creation system in the history of the world.

This is pretty dramatic stuff, and the rhetorical strategy is to enable the mass of outrageous commitments to overwhelm. The sheer quantity of claims, combined with the intensity of outrage that they provoke, takes on an exasperating quality of its own.

In all these cases, the effect is not only that audiences are distracted from the actual views proposed by the other side, they are also prevented from even hearing those views in their non-distorted forms. In repudiating opponents as if they are all cut from the same untenable and hapless cloth of ridiculous views, further exchange with them is foreclosed. More importantly, the façade of argument is employed as a way to mug to one's allies. This in turn strokes their in-group biases, leading inevitably to the polarization that was discussed in the previous chapter.

Memeology

Contemporary political discourse supplies all too many examples of merely simulated argument. One of the most egregious forms that this argumentative pathology of simulated argument is manifested in political memes. And the evolution of particular memes reflects how ardently some disputants refuse to engage each other. Consider the trajectory of the Pepe the Frog meme. By our lights, the meme's evolution has taken three stages: the Pepe stage, the NPC stage, and the Honkler stage. We presume that it will continue to evolve as the political landscape changes, or others will arise in its place. But the trajectory of the Pepe meme is indicative of the problems of argumentative engagement when the sides are deeply entrenched.

Pepe the Frog, initially, was a symbol for doing what "feels good, man," but it became an alt-right icon reflecting consternation in the face of what was portrayed as an excessive and decadent liberal culture. It was regularly deployed as a reaction to perceived left-wing hypocrisy or negative reactions from progressives when conservative ideas are voiced. Pepe would be portrayed with a sad face, saying "feels bad, man" in response to some new outrage of progressive politics. Pepe would appear with a smug face when pointing out how some social justice initiative suffers from inconsistency or an opponent has clearly overreacted to criticism. Pepe's political deployment had racist usage, too. Pepe heads are regularly superimposed on bodies of Nazis, and Pepe is frequently portrayed as happily committing acts of violence against a minority. The meme became very popular during the 2016 presidential election. And after candidate Donald Trump tweeted a picture of himself with green Pepe skin, the meme had truly arrived.

In the wake of Trump's election victory, the Pepe meme morphed into portraying the opposition to Trump as unthinking and scripted.

This was an important view for the alt-right supporters of Trump, as his critics persistently charge him with racism, flagrant disregard for democratic norms, and general dishonesty. The response from certain Trump supporters is to claim that these supposed allegations are mere talking points, noise intended to undermine the president. Thus, the NPC meme was born. NPC stands for *Non-Player Character*, a term taken from gaming culture for characters in video games controlled exclusively by the computer – characters with no purpose beyond being things for players to interact with, typically for information or resources. They are the human-shaped furniture of a gaming world.

The NPC meme depicts Trump's critics as empty-headed programs, mere obstacles without minds, devoid of reason. The NPC image is of a blank-faced gray head; the NPCs usually come in groups, all saying the same thing in mindless uniformity. "Orange man bad," is their catch phrase. And so, any line of criticism of Trump is placed in the mouths of the NPCs with this phrase to punctuate it. This signals to Trump's supporters that the alleged criticism is mindless claptrap and thus nothing to listen to, much less respond to.

A telling element to this meme is its solipsism. Those who call others NPCs imply that they themselves are the true *players,* the only ones in the conversation with minds that reflect and understand. Think of the narcissism at the core of this thought. One must be certain that one is right about so many things for this to be an appealing way to think of others with whom one disagrees. Think further about what it would take for one to say it out loud to those others. One would have to think the following: *either they don't have views at all, or their views simply don't matter*. Either way, the implication is that one's take on the situation is the only thing worth saying. But the problem arises – *who else* is really a player? Are you alone in this game, surrounded only by NPCs? Even those who say the same things as you could be programmed to do so. Once invested in this line of thought, you have retreated to a form of *solipsism* – thinking that you are the only thing that is or that matters. The trouble is that this viewpoint is clearly self-defeating as a *political* viewpoint, since its message must be of the form: *since solipsism is true, more people should be solipsists.*

The third stage of the Pepe meme is the Honk! meme, or Pepe the Honkler. In this case, Pepe has a red clown nose and rainbow hair. He holds a small bicycle horn, and every time the NPCs or liberals say something, Pepe the clown honks his horn. The *Honk!* symbolizes the bemused astonishment at the absurdity of liberal politics. Pepe the Honkler typifies the troll's perspective on disagreement – arguing is pointless, as those with whom one disagrees are too far gone, they embody a "clown world." The Honkler is supposed to be a full-throated laugh in the face of the decline of civilization. It is not a tragedy, but a comedy.

The problem, of course, is that the memes are tactics by which the alt-right expresses its collective disgust with liberals, or "the Left," now depicted as so depraved as to be not merely wrong, but utterly unintelligible. Not even having minds, in the end. At the same time, these memes also present strong inducements for in-group conformity. As we saw earlier, this secures the conditions for belief polarization. And in any case, these are instances where one side to a political dispute promulgates images of their opponents as less than human; this is antithetical to the civility that is central to the ideal of a democratic society. Memes are satisfying, but they are so only because they are empty mimics of appropriate criticism.

7

Fake News

"Whoever wears the shoes knows best where they pinch." This adage is sometimes offered as a consideration in support of democracy. Basically, the idea is that the citizens should rule because they're the ones who will feel the impact of the government's laws and policies. Being "on the ground" gives the people insight into what needs doing and how the government is performing, insights that detached policymakers are unlikely to have. It's an ennobling image, to be sure. However, it's also simplistic. Matters of public policy are notoriously complex, and their impacts are not usefully characterized as a "pinch" on the heel of the body politic. When assessing the fit of a shoe, one needs only to check how comfortable they are. Political issues are different in kind. They invoke questions of fairness, freedom, equality, and justice. Often, policies that best fit those requirements are not the most comfortable; for example, fairness can "pinch" too, especially if you've become used to getting more than your fair share. In that case, equality often feels like something unfair for those with unacknowledged advantages. So, whatever its other merits might be, the adage is limited in this way.

But there's another crucial respect in which democratic self-government is unlike feeling a pinch. In large-scale societies, it is inevitable that the business of democracy is conducted at a distance from the citizenry. Accordingly, the idea that the assessment of political matters could be enacted in some *direct* way, as when a person asks a clerk at a shoe store for a larger size, is unrealistic. That is, modern democracy is highly *mediated*. The mechanisms of political representation are but one aspect of the mediated nature of democracy. The *media* is another site of political mediation.

This is as it should be. The task of government is a full-time job, and our political representatives rely upon an expansive set of institutions and a complex division of labor. No office holder governs alone. Similarly, in order to do our job as democratic citizens, we must rely on others. In particular, we rely on journalists and reporters – in general, the Press – to help provide information that can guide our political judgments. Citizens cannot themselves "go to the source" and find out first-hand what's going on in Congress or the White House. In order to govern ourselves responsibly, we need to be able to disagree civilly; but this means that we need access to the kind of information that could *inform* our arguments. A responsible and reliable free Press is therefore central to democracy.

But there's the problem, right? Think of the chilling vision presented in George Orwell's *1984* of a society intellectually enslaved by its news media. And we know real-world cases in which authoritarian governments have successfully used the Press as a tool for propaganda. Citizens are provided with what is presented as *information* for them to include in their deliberations, but what is, in fact, indoctrination. These are instances of simulated argument writ large, scaled-up for an entire society.

In recent years, the term "fake news" has been introduced into our political vocabulary. To call something "fake" is to criticize it as being counterfeit or inauthentic. Despite the depth of disagreements over other political matters, there's widespread agreement that fake news is a problem for democracy. Perhaps it should not be surprising that this agreement obtains in the absence of a clear analysis of what fake news is. The consensus that fake news is a problem may itself rely on that ambiguity. That is, the consensus might come to nothing more than this: whatever fake news is, it's a problem.

That's an instance of what philosophers call a *merely verbal* agreement. Such agreements look substantial, when in fact they're merely ways to stifle disagreements with words. Think of a group of people all discussing a matter over which they disagree; after some period of time, they emerge with the good news that they've reached the agreement that they'll all "do the right thing" in response to the subject of their dispute. It's hardly ever the case that anyone would describe the action they believe they should take as being the *wrong thing* to do, so when a group agrees to "do the right thing," they've not really agreed on anything. Whatever disagreements they might have concerning *what the right thing is* remain unaddressed. Still, there are cases in which merely verbal agreements are satisfactory. They can serve as a kind of truce among divided people, enabling them to get along. Not every unstable apple cart needs to be upset.

But the possibility that the consensus over fake news is merely verbal is unsettling. This is because the charge of "fake news" tends to be *politically opportunistic*, that is, aimed at delegitimating a story that has been reported as news, while also criticizing the person or agency doing the reporting. Not only is the news fake, but the reporter is a fake, too. But nothing much else is clear from this. What makes it fake, and how is it different from merely being false? Having a precise definition of what constitutes fake news is needed in order to distinguish actual instances of fake news from the cases in which the charge of fake news is invoked in this merely opportunistic way.

What is Fake News?

Let's begin with an intuitive view. Whatever else might be involved, fake news attempts to deceive by means of communication. This suggests three components. First, fake news is a kind of communication; specifically, it involves *reportage*. Second, as fake news aims to deceive, it involves reportage of what is false (or at least misleading). Third, as authentic news sources can report what is misleading (due to honest journalistic error, for example), fake news must involve an *intention* to mislead. Tying these together, fake news is *intentionally misleading reportage*. To tighten things up further, add that fake news is the reportage *as news* of content that is intentionally misleading.

This simple definition looks promising. In fact, we think it captures the concept of fake news as it is popularly understood. It's effectively the charge of lying, but lying as a representative of the media. That's an intuitive and powerful charge. However, the analysis is lacking. There are instances of fake news that are nonetheless excluded by the definition. Consider the following:

CRIME REPORT: A putative news Source reports (accurately) to an Audience an Incident in which a violent crime is committed within the Audience's vicinity, by a group identified as Muslim immigrants.

Thus far, the original definition delivers the right result: there is no fake news. But let's add that in CRIME REPORT the Source *excessively* reports the Incident throughout a news cycle, *underreports* cases of similar crimes committed by people who are not immigrants, and reports the Incident in a manner that could give a casual member of the Audience the impression that *several distinct* crimes involving Muslim immigrants have taken place. Nonetheless, the Source's reportage involves no fabricated information and no misleading reports; in fact, the reportage accurately depicts the Incident.

Yet CRIME REPORT is clearly an instance of fake news. The Source's reportage is misleading in a straightforward way, but not because of the content of what's reported. It's misleading because of what the Audience is expected to do with what's reported. We are vulnerable to what is known as the *availability heuristic*; that is, we are prone to think that the ease with which we can think of an instance in which some kind of event has occurred tracks the probability of that kind of event occurring. In brief, the easier it is for you to recall a shark attack, the more common you think shark attacks are. So, the constant repetition of the reporting of the Incident leads the Audience to infer that crimes of that kind are especially common. Note that the availability heuristic need not involve the creation of *new beliefs*; the repeated report can be misleading in that it confirms or fortifies existing beliefs prevalent in the Audience.

Consider next a second kind of case:

WEBSITE TRAFFIC: A person seeks to maximize revenue produced by his website. He finds that posting fabricated accounts of lurid conspiracies involving prominent politicians reliably increases site traffic, which in turn enables him to sell ads at high rates. So he regularly posts content of that kind.

Suppose further that this person does not intend to mislead anyone, but only to maximize revenue. Stipulate in addition that he would be sincerely *surprised* to discover that visitors tend to believe his outrageous posts. Perhaps he regards his site as a source of sardonic entertainment, and so denies that it presents content *as news*. Still, visitors tend to regard his site as an authentic news source, and accept what he posts as fact. Our proprietor has none of the intentions or motives required by our initial definition, but this nonetheless is a case of fake news.

It's not difficult to construct further examples that intuitively look like fake news in which the initial definition (intentionally misleading reportage presented as news) is nonetheless not satisfied. A more nuanced conception of fake news is required.

An Institutional View

We think that such a conception begins with a shift in emphasis away from *reports* or the presentation of *particular bits of information* and toward the operation of *institutions* that pose as sources of information for citizens. We propose as an alternative an "institutional" account of fake news. It says that "fake news" characterizes the activities of institutions that pose as journalistic, which by design feed and codify the *antecedent biases* of a preselected audience by exploiting their vulnerabilities (cognitive and otherwise), all with a view to facilitating some decidedly political objective.

That's admittedly a mouthful. But notice that the institutional conception captures what's going wrong in cases like CRIME REPORT. The issue there is not, after all, false reporting or the presentation of fabrication as fact. The problem resides rather with the general *structure* of the reportage. In particular, the "fake news" lies in the overall tendency to repeat certain factual statements and omit others, strategically deployed to fit the expectations and preferences of a target audience of citizens. Note also that the institutional view enables us to identify how the dysfunction in CRIME REPORT is distinct from other instances of public disinformation; since it can allow for fake news that involves no inaccurate reportage, it can distinguish fake news from, say, garden-variety propaganda.

Look now at WEBSITE TRAFFIC. Here, it is not the proprietor's *intention* to mislead the public; that's not what he's about. Rather, his intention is to maximize website revenue, and it so happens that he can best achieve the aim he intends by promulgating political conspiracy theories online. Nonetheless, his enterprise counts as fake news because his reports pose as journalistic and are designed to play on the political biases and anxieties of his audience, with a view toward keeping their attention and feeding their desire for political messaging that fortifies their preexisting attitudes concerning the political opposition. So, even though he does not take himself to be engaged in a political disinformation campaign, and thus does not have the relevant *intentions* to mislead, he is nonetheless producing fake news.

Perhaps the most important feature of our institutional view, though, is that it focuses attention on a feature of fake news that the initial definition tends to obscure or downplay. Note that the initial definition attends almost exclusively on the *purveyors* of fake news, the "outlets" producing fake news. Fake news is then understood as a kind of disinformation campaign perpetrated against the public at large. It is in this sense strictly a *supply side* account of the phenomenon. But fake news also calls for a *demand side* analysis. After all, infamous fake news cases in the US – like Pizzagate, Birtherism, and the report that Sarah Palin once referred to Africa as a country – *all* play to the biases, anxieties, and vulnerabilities of *pre-identified* audiences. The same goes in Britain for the report, put out by the Vote Leave campaign before the 2016 Brexit referendum, that the UK pays £350 million per week to the EU. Or that prior to the vote, Vote Leave was warning of Turkey's drag on the EU economy (the problem was that Turkey is not part of the EU). Indeed, in all these cases, audiences are often *self-selected*; they *elect* to visit the websites, and tune-in to the programs. Fake news is always *targeted*, not at the general populace, but rather at a specific segment of the citizenry.

The Demand for Fake News

And here we find a bleak truth lurking. The disturbing proliferation of fake news and its political impact is made possible by the fact that contemporary democratic citizens *want to be assured that their political opponents are not simply mistaken, but also craven*. It's not enough to believe that a political opponent is flatly *wrong*, citizens now seek out ways to believe them to be also criminal, depraved, incompetent, and incapable. What is more, thanks to new communications technologies, citizens can *express that desire for confirmation* in market-effective ways. They can press the *demand* for satisfying content, and *reward* those who produce it. Were it not for the demand for fake news, there would not be so much of it. In this sense, fake news is as much the *product* of our dysfunctional argumentative culture as it is among its causes.

Hence we see how fake news figures in the more general phenomenon we introduced in our discussion of polarization in Chapter 4. Recall that the polarization dynamic involves the interplay between two forces that are both called polarization: *political* polarization refers to the ideological distance between opposing political camps, and *belief* polarization refers to the phenomenon by which people who share a common social identity become more extreme advocates of the views that are characteristic of their identity group.

The dynamic consists in the mutual reinforcement of these two forces: as we belief-polarize, we find those with whom we disagree increasingly unintelligible, and so we come to regard them as not worth engaging with; this in turn leads us to interact only with people who are politically just like ourselves, which enforces the in-group homogeneity of political polarization, while stimulating further belief polarization. Eventually, politically opposed camps grow and are unable to interact productively; they actually come to regard the other side as unfit for citizenship. Fake news, in the institutional sense we have described here, helps to drive this dynamic by supplying partisans with a steady intake of reinforcing depictions of the other side as fitting the distortions that the polarization dynamic projects. In the end, civil political disagreement is rendered impossible, since citizens are convinced that their opposition is so depraved that there's nothing in their divisions that rises to the level of a *disagreement* at all. Each side comes to see the other as simply making noise.

The War for Your Mind

US radio host Alex Jones's *InfoWars* website is posited on the thesis that all other institutions informing the American populace produce fake news. The catchphrase of Jones's organization is: "There is a war on for your mind!" The irony, of course, is that *InfoWars* itself is a source and repeater of many fake news stories. Jones did not believe that the Sandy Hook mass shooting was real; he was a believer and propagator of the Pizzagate conspiracy, according to which then presidential candidate Hillary Clinton was implicated in a child sex ring run out of a pizza parlor. Yet Jones uses the term "fake news" to rebut any negative reporting on the Trump White House. The lesson is that, in the hands of partisans, the accusation of fake news is no longer a term for evaluating information or reportage, but is simply a tool for rejecting an interlocutor's claims.

The point of developing a set of tools for critical thinking and argument evaluation is that we try to work out impartial criteria for analyzing our reasoning. We try to identify a set of standards to which we can hold ourselves and others. When we reason, we do so in our natural language, and so we reason about cats, money, lumbermills, and people. But to reason about our reasoning, we need a vocabulary about how that reasoning is going. Particular patterns of reasons emerge that are worth noting. For example, the following arguments are of the same form, even though they are about radically different things:

This is a triangle only if it has three sides, and it does not have three sides; so it is not a triangle.

You can graduate only if you take a writing class, and you have not taken a writing class; so you cannot graduate.

The faucet will run only if the water is turned on, and the water is not turned on; so the faucet will not run.

To capture the notion that there's a special pattern to all these different arguments, which is itself the same regardless of whether we are talking about triangles, graduation, or faucets, we need a *metalanguage* – a language about how we are using language to reason about those things. The name given to that shared form of reasoning in the examples above is *modus tollens* – a method of negating something by negating another thing. You already speak many metalanguages, by the way. Grammar is a metalanguage, as the notion of nouns, verbs, and their agreement isn't about the things we talk about; rather, it's about how we talk about the things we talk about. That's what makes it a *meta*language. The same goes for literary criticism, with the notion of rhymes and metaphors; there are also speech codes, with the notions of profanity and slurs. The vocabulary of logic is a metalanguage in that same sense – it's a language about how we use language to argue.

The key, again, is that the vocabulary of the metalanguage of logic is supposed to be a tool for arbitrating disputes about what we disagree over and how the reasons work. So we have the notion of a good inference, sufficient evidence, and the idea of fallacies and doubletalk. *Fake news* is a new addition to that critical vocabulary, and we've tried to define how it describes repeatable patterns of sharing information that systematically misleads audiences. But one thing to note is that the term "fake news" is not now used as a tool for impartial arbitration when it comes to evaluating arguments and information. It is used in a way that is equivalent to rejecting reports one simply disagrees with or that one finds to have an overtone that one finds objectionable. The *metalanguage has been weaponized* to be yet one more smear on the other side's views and expressions. It is likely that this is the trajectory of all critical metalanguages – that, if they are used to arbitrate disputes, they will be used by the disputants strategically and ultimately abused. This is the trajectory of the notion of fake news – it described a pattern of misleading reporting as a means of correcting an element of the exchange, but it has been put to the service of being another strategy of repudiation.

8

Deep Disagreements

In a normal disagreement, opposing sides share enough common ground for them to agree on what it would take to resolve the dispute. So those who disagree about who won the 1986 World Cup can look it up on the FIFA website; if there's a dispute concerning the best route home, they can consult a map. Typically, disagreements progress against a shared conception of what would count as a resolution. But what about disagreements where disputants have no such background agreement? Let us call these *deep* disagreements. In deep disagreements, disputants are divided not only over the facts, but also over the criteria for determining what the facts are.[1] And, as we saw in previous chapters, persistent disagreement easily slides from a purely intellectual exercise into all-out emotional combat. It is very easy to bear contempt for those with whom one has significant disagreement, and it is easy to see why. Deep disagreements threaten our identities.

Given the requirement that political disagreements manifest our commitment to the political equality of our interlocutors, conducting ourselves civilly in contexts of deep disagreement can be difficult.

---

1   See Robert Fogelin's "The Logic of Deep Disagreements," in *Informal Logic* (1985) 7:1, for this distinction between normal and deep disagreements and an argument that deep disagreements are not rationally resolvable.

Here, we outline a few problems unique to deep disagreements and offer some methods for managing them.

Deep Disagreements and the Good, Bad, News

The problem of deep disagreement is that of finding a way to argue with someone with whom you do not share background commitments sufficient to resolve the issue. The arguments you give will employ premises that they reject, and arguments they give you will have premises that will strike you as unacceptable or irrelevant. In such cases, it seems as if rational discourse cannot prevail.

Despite the fact that deep disagreement presents a problem for civil disagreement, we should pause to note that the fact that there are deep disagreements is actually a good thing. This is what we think is the good, bad, news about deep disagreements. Here's the bad news: deep disagreements are significant challenges to rational resolution for issues of significance. They plague us. Here's the good news: that there are deep disagreements is an indication of the robustness of the intellectual freedoms we exercise. Imagine a polity where there is no deep disagreement, and all agree on fundamental truths about human beings, justice, knowledge, and meaning. Where there are no deep disagreements, but only normal disagreements, everything's resolvable. Imagine that there are no *deep disagreements* about all the things you care about, a complete consensus around your views. That sounds nice, doesn't it? But when we look more carefully, it's maybe not so nice. Ask yourself: under those conditions, would your beliefs be based on evidence and reason or simply on social conditioning? Further, ask yourself how someone under those conditions would be handled were they to disagree with the consensus. Finally, ask yourself whether you, having been exposed to so many alien ideas and knowing where the criticisms (even if misguided) of these ideas are, would be welcome in that society. Our concern is that a society without deep disagreement can be maintained only under conditions of significant social and intellectual control. Societies that have no intellectual diversity reek of repressed freedoms, and in any case do not respect political equality. So let's emphasize something positive about deep disagreements: they are testament to the fact that intellectual freedoms are protected and exercised among political equals. So, that's the good, bad, news about deep disagreements: they themselves are significant challenges, but that they exist is an indicator of a kind of health in a polity.

It's not a surprise, really. Under the conditions of intellectual freedom that democracy secures for its citizens, we would expect a proliferation of diverse and conflicting viewpoints. Ongoing disagreement of a variety of depths is a byproduct of democracy working properly. The problem is that when disagreement persists and runs deep, disputants can grow bitter and come to resent the intellectual freedom of their opponents. So, despite the fact that deep disagreements reflect the good news of intellectual freedom, it bodes ill for the things those freedoms were cultivated to promote – namely, civil political disagreement.

So one irony of deep disagreements is that they emerge out of our intellectual freedom and political equality, but they then can threaten that freedom and equality. An additional irony is that deep disagreement, as the problem it manifests as a problem of argument, is actually a direct product of our commitment to civility in disagreement. Here's how that second irony occurs. It's a norm of civil disagreement that you should present arguments that contain premises that not only *you* but also your *audience* can accept and regard as supporting the conclusion. That is, arguments have a self-regarding face (representing your reasons) and an other-regarding face (presenting those reasons to another person who has questions, disagrees, etc.). The hope is that when you give people your reasons, they will endorse those reasons and make them their own. In the end, we would have shared reasons, *our reasons.* Call this particular norm of civility the *dialecticality norm.*

The dialecticality norm calls for us to regard our fellow citizens as *partners in reasoning,* fellow reasoners to whom our arguments are addressed. Now we can see that deep disagreements arise when the two sides of a dispute cannot live up to the dialecticality requirement. Neither side can offer reasons in support of their respective position that the other side could regard *as reasons.* The problem of deep disagreement, then, is born of the aspiration of civil disagreement. If we weren't out to be civil about our disagreements, and in being civil, live up to the norm of dialecticality, then deep disagreements wouldn't be the problem of argument it is.

Once again, deep disagreement provides us with some good, bad, news. Not only does it reflect political arrangements wherein we have the freedom to think and argue according to our best lights, but it also emerges out of a shared commitment to dialecticality. That's the good news. In fact, that we are so troubled and frustrated by deep disagreement is yet another piece of good news. The frustration indicates the depth of our commitment to civility, even where there is especially severe disagreement. The problem is that, despite all this good news about the health of our democratic norms and our commitment to civility and dialecticality, there is the bad news that we have deep disagreements to manage.

Charity and Disagreement

Still, deep disagreements present a problem for democracy. At its core, the problem lies in how shared reasons can arise from disputes between people who seem to share none. It may seem hopeless, but one place to start is with the claim that there are some disputes in which participants share *no reasons at all*. Despite the fact that there is great diversity in our beliefs, that diversity might never be so drastic as to give rise to disagreements that are *absolutely deep*.

Consider some claims that, we assume, will strike you as truisms: human life is valuable, intelligence is worth honoring, stability for the future is important, and dignity is something to be preserved. In political disagreements, despite the depth of the divides, most are conducted against a backdrop of broader agreement concerning these and other truisms, where we agree on these generalities, but perhaps differ on what counts as dignity, or how to identify intelligence, or when human life begins and ends. To portray disagreement as so deep that the sides share *nothing at all* in common is to fail to properly understand the dispute. The two sides regard each other as *disagreeing*, after all. That's something about which they agree.

This interpretive point is a lesson in the *principle of charity*. The principle holds that the best interpretation of others will be the one that attributes to them the greatest proportion of true commitments or one that interprets their claims in ways that maximize the other side's rationality. You interpret others in ways that puts them in better lights, not worse. The reason why the principle is a good rule to follow is simply that if we interpreted others to have nothing but false beliefs or that they are manifestly terrible reasoners about everything, it would be very difficult to make sense of what they are doing or what their words even mean. If we didn't see others as having mostly true beliefs and reasoning pretty reliably, they would simply be unintelligible to us. And so, the reality is that in order for two people to get to the point where they recognize that they have a deep political disagreement, they must nevertheless have a wide background of agreement, too. Otherwise, they would not be able to see each other's commitments or proposals as meaningful at all. In order for you to *disagree* with someone, you have to think the things they said are *false* or that their reasoning is *bad* – if you can't recognize their claims as meaningful at all or you don't see their reasoning as reasoning at all, you can't even reject it as false or fallacious. The principle of charity rules out cases of disagreements where the parties share absolutely *no* commitments. Nothing that could count as a disagreement can run *that* deep.

Further, in order for us to see a disagreement as *deep*, we must, in fact, know quite a bit about the reasons our opponents use. We cannot just start with their *conclusions* and judge the disagreement as deep; rather, we must see how and from what they reason. This is an important stipulation, since it is tempting, when hearing about a view one rejects, to pronounce those who hold it to be not worth arguing with. In the same way that *pseudoreasoning* is picking one's conclusion and arranging one's premises and authorities to support it, so *pseudocriticism* begins with rejecting an opponent's conclusion and then holding their arguments as bad, since they lead to a conclusion one doesn't hold. The principle of charity exists to prevent us from performing this pseudocritical move – we must work to reconstruct and understand the arguments of our opponents. Again, anything that counts as disagreement must involve the possibility of each side achieving an understanding of the other side's reasoning.

Notice that if we reject the dialecticality norm either in not addressing our arguments to those with whom we disagree or in not reconstructing and criticizing their actual arguments, we refuse to treat these others as equal partners in reasoning. Either way, we are opting out of the project of sharing reasons. *And once we no longer take the norm of dialecticality to bind our arguments, it is virtually guaranteed that our arguments will look like nonsense to the other side.* When one stops trying to hear one's opponents as rational or address them as capable reasoners, it shows. It manifests as a display of contempt, and, from their perspective, it makes for a very badly formed argument. We now can see why there is a vicious cycle of contemptuous and bad arguments.

Calling Disagreements "Deep"

It is important with a concept like that of *deep disagreement* that we are careful with its application. The big reason is that misapplying the term has effects on how we approach the arguments we might have with the other side. Prematurely calling a disagreement *deep* can stand in the way of our attempts at what would be otherwise straightforward normal solutions. Perhaps this has happened to you before with some problem – you take a few shots at solving it, you fail, and you infer that the problem must be impossible to solve. That's what threatens to happen with the concept of deep disagreement – a few cases of argument not resolving the issue does not a deep disagreement make. Just because critical conversation is taking a while and is frustrating does not mean that the gap is not bridgeable or that the other side has too far gone. Sometimes, it takes extensive reasoning to get to the bottom of things.

Prematurely taking a disagreement as deep, beyond missing the more direct method of resolving the issue, also primes us for potentially bad arguments. The primary reason for that is that instances of deep disagreement regularly involve us in not even engaging with the other side, but rather in shoring up one's agreements with the undecided participants. The result is that, as the dialecticality norm gets dropped, it becomes unclear how the two opposed views actually critically bear on each other.

Philosophical debates might be a good model for handling deep disagreements. The disagreements bear on concepts that are part of our background assumptions that run our lives, and the criteria for accepting or rejecting our fundamental commitments are as controversial as the commitments. A philosophical disagreement arises when we have the freedom to pursue our disputes to the competing concepts or orientations that generate them. As the clash of concepts becomes progressively more fundamental, the disagreement seems proportionately deeper. And so debates about whether there is free will hinge on what *freedom* really is, and debates about whether there can be morally obligatory lies hinge on what our fundamental moral duties really are. As disagreements get deeper, they get more philosophical. Now, if we see things that way, deep disagreements are hard problems that arise when we can reflect on our closely held commitments and puzzle why others don't hold them too. But the key is that deep disagreements in philosophy are never *absolutely deep*. Philosophers work, even when they disagree, to jointly keep track of their exchanges, to relate their conflicting reasons to others that have some hope of being shared, and so on. What defines a philosophical dispute is not just the concepts that are at issue with it, but also the ones that are not at issue. And so, when we ask whether God can make a rock so heavy He can't move it (a paradox of omnipotence), the concept of *movement* stays put. And when we ask whether lies can ever be morally obligatory, we work to make sure we keep the notion of a *lie* continuous. This isn't just for the sake of arranging the tools for the ongoing debate; it's also for the sake of understanding what the debate is about. If the two sides in the debate over whether lies can ever be morally obligatory also had significant disagreements over what lies are, it's hard to see what the debate really is about in the first place.

The lesson, then, is that the depth of deep disagreements is ripe for hyperbole. Yes, there are disagreements of significant depth, but for us to see them as disagreements at all, they cannot be disagreements of absolute depth. And, in light of that, it's worth remembering that disagreements are best thought of not just in terms of the matters at issue, but the matters that both sides take as settled.

Depths of Disagreement

Even if there can be no disagreements with *absolute* depth, there nevertheless are *severely* deep disagreements, cases where disputants can see no way forward toward rational resolution of their disagreement. How should we handle them? To start, we don't think there is a solution to the problem of such disagreement. As we've shown, the possibility of deep disagreement emerges out of commitments to intellectual freedom and political equality; it is better to sustain than to reject these commitments, even if keeping them means facing deep disagreements. The problem posed by deep disagreements is the price of freedom and equality. That said, there are still ways to mitigate deep disagreements.

It's reasonable to say that the deeper the disagreement gets, the harder it is to argue at all. But that's a far cry from saying that there could be a depth to disagreement that would render argument strictly *impossible*. Argument is surely possible under conditions of severely deep disagreement. What's more, when confronting an especially deep disagreement, disputants can still reason together about the depth of the disagreement itself. They can identify its boundaries, ascertain its sources, and even agree that their deep disagreement be kept from infecting their other, less deep, disagreements. Consider instances where you and someone else "agree to disagree" about an issue of significance, but you still have to get on together over many other things. You both know the limits of the disagreement, how it may inform the other person's life in a variety of ways, and they may see that with you, too. But you find ways to avoid the topic, or, if you must address it, you can even announce that you're not going to change their minds on *this* topic, but maybe there's room on some *other topic* that you can talk about. We've all had neighbors with whom we have significant political disagreements, but we can still have perfectly robust exchanges about a variety of things, either skirting the deeper disagreement or jointly acknowledging it and moving on. That's standard stuff for grownups, isn't it? Well, that's one way we nevertheless reason *about deep disagreements*, even when we can't make much progress reasoning *in them*.

A further method for managing deep disagreements is to note that, although we may *begin* the disagreement in positions where we do not share much, civil dialogue itself might change that. In fact, it's a common result of well-conducted critical exchange that participants achieve a more reliable sense of the strength of their reasons. They often see fit to revise their commitments in the wake of civil exchange. Earlier, we distinguished the *patient* and the *partner* models for argument (see Chapter 6). The *patient* model holds that those with whom we argue must be diagnosed and then provided with a corrective – arguing is something we *do to* them. On the *partner* model, those with whom we argue are equal sources of reasons and critical views – arguing, then, is something we *do with* them. Deep disagreements look impassible on the patient model, because it sees argument as always beginning from the fixed starting points of each interlocutor. The partner model allows for the *revision* of our initial premises, thus permitting new sites of agreement to emerge from argumentative exchange.

Think of your own intellectual growth – how you've evolved on an issue. You might once have thought that some viewpoint was ridiculous and that the reasons for it were worse. But defenders of that view heard your pushback, they revised the view, sharpened the reasons, and got back to you. Your view about their view changed. And maybe, then, your own view about the views you held earlier changed. We are not intellectually static beings, and deep disagreements, when handled properly, needn't *remain* deep. The key is to remember that when it comes to disagreements over things that are important, resolution is sometimes a long way off. But we are adults, and we are up for hard conversations.

The real challenge facing our approach is that the partnership model is a not an easy fit with the emotional reactions we commonly have toward those with whom we deeply disagree. In deep disagreements, we don't just see the other side as simply wrong, but as deeply so. And that cognitive assessment invokes a moral assessment with an emotional affect. It's hard to partner with others in argument if you think them not just in error, but as bad people. Are they deserving of civil political disagreement?

Why adopt the partnership model of argument with them? Why be civil at all when so much is on the line? We can take steps to resolve deep disagreements if we adopt the thought that we're all equals and we all deserve reasons to be given to us that we understand and our reasons are heard – yes; but it's very tempting to reject the partnership model because it requires we open ourselves to critique from people and views we disdain. So, we ask: how can a culture of partnership in argument be saved when we have deep disagreements?

9

Civility as a Reciprocal Virtue

All our talk thus far about civil political disagreement and the need to argue well might look great on paper, but isn't it really just too pie-in-the-sky? After all, everyone knows what political disagreement in the real world looks like: name-calling, hectoring, dissembling, browbeating, intimidation, mobbing, and worse. And real-world democracy has little to do with collective inquiry and seeking the truth; it's rather a mostly peaceful but nonetheless often ruthless struggle for power. So no matter how attractive our depiction of the ideal of democratic citizenship may be, it's nothing more than an academic fantasy. Real politics simply isn't like that.

We are aware of the state of democratic politics in the real world. Notice, however, that hardly anyone *embraces* this status quo. When people describe politics in such terms, they are most often *complaining*. Everyone expresses disappointment with the way things are. To be sure, the democratic ideal will never be fully realized. But that's precisely the nature of an *ideal*, after all – it identifies an aspiration. Indeed, our lamentations over the pervasive nastiness and incivility in politics make sense as *complaints* only against the backdrop of an aspirational alternative. True, our conception of civil disagreement might be pie-in-the-sky. But the alternative is to embrace the status quo, to see it as *proper*. That invites further deterioration. Sometimes, in order to merely sustain a suboptimal status quo, we need to uphold a distant ideal.

It bears repeating that our ideal of civil political disagreement hasn't simply been plucked from thin air. It expresses a collection of aspirations that are built into democracy. The significance of that claim shouldn't be understated. When people talk about saving democracy, they talk about how some contingent feature of the world has brought about democracy's downfall – and all that's necessary is that we change that contingent fact. Lots of non-ideal theory works this way. One points to some pervasive, but contingent, feature of a society – be it racism, economic disparity, or corruption – then one shows how that feature should be changed. Our view, as ideal theory, diverges pretty significantly from that way of proceeding. First, as we said earlier, you can't theorize the way in which democracy is failing in some way or another unless you've got a notion of how it ought to function to begin with. But second, and most importantly, our view is that some of democracy's failings arise not because of some bad distribution of wealth or systematic bigotry (which, we do agree, both obtain and contribute to democratic pathology), but rather because democracy contains within itself a vulnerability that cannot be completely overcome. Our view is that democracy is an intrinsically conflicted and discordant political arrangement; by its nature, democracy invites certain political pathologies. To see both of these points, we must first understand the ideals of democracy, see them clearly, and recognize that the background of shared argument and civil engagement is what makes the problem manifest.

What's more, despite the shameful condition of our current politics, the ideals of civil political disagreement and their corresponding public virtues are widely appealed to in political commentary. Real-world democracy might come to little more than a struggle for power, but we nevertheless hold one another to higher standards of civil conduct. For example, when the president characterizes those he perceives to be his critics as "very dishonest people," he appeals to the public virtue of honesty. And when he charges his political opponents of being simply motivated by "political gain," he appeals to the public virtue of civic-mindedness. Charges of bias and partiality uphold the related public virtue of evenhandedness. When one criticizes a news organization – be it MSNBC, Fox News, *The New York Times*, or *The Wall Street Journal* – for being slanted or a mere bullhorn for a singular partisan perspective, one is insisting upon a public virtue of fairness. Note, too, that it is common now for the word "partisanship" to be used as a criticism; when one official charges another with being "partisan," she is claiming that the other is acting in a way that is unresponsive to the reasons in play, dogmatically committed to a party line. Such charges uphold the ideal of civil disagreement we have been developing. The fact is that real-world politics, warts and all, is awash with calls to public virtue, the dispositions appropriate for democratic citizens. You can't understand the details of real-world politics without understanding the ideals invoked and then subverted by its practitioners.

This occasions a puzzle. We all uphold the same democratic ideals and value the same public virtues. So why is politics so debased? Call this the *debasement puzzle*. To unravel it, we must first examine the *structure* of public virtue.

Reciprocal Public Virtues

Let's start by distinguishing public virtues that are *first-personal* and those that are *reciprocal*. An analogy with garden-variety moral virtue will be helpful. Consider a virtue like *moderation*. This virtue establishes a standard of conduct that requires of the individual temperance in the pursuit of enjoyment. This standard is *first-personal*. What it requires is not contingent on the presence of other temperate people; the virtue of temperance *applies* to individuals as individuals, and demands of them individual moderation, even in the presence of immoderate company. No matter how indulgent others might be, each of us should be moderate. Importantly, when one is among indulgent others, the virtue of moderation might even require a *greater degree* of temperance.

Another first-personal virtue is *courage*. The courageous person stands firm in fearful situations. Even when surrounded by cowards, the virtue of courage calls one to hold steady. To be sure, precisely *what* course of action courage requires might depend on one's company and what they are currently doing. For example, courage does not require that one stand alone against an opposing army after all one's cowardly comrades have run away. That is to say, courage does not call for one to stand firm *no matter what*; it does not require *rashness* in the face of fear. Nonetheless, that others are cowards does not license anything less than courage from the courageous person. Again, courage, as a first-personal virtue, applies to the individual.

Now contrast these first-personal virtues with moral virtues of a different kind. These virtues do not primarily attach to individuals, but they instead govern *groups* of individuals or are exhibited in relations between them. That is, they establish a standard of conduct for *us* rather than simply for *me* and *you*. Here's a playground example. We teach children the policy "keep your hands to yourself," and in order to refer to those who stably embody this norm, we can fabricate a term for the corresponding virtue. Let's say that a child who exhibits the stable disposition to keep his hands to himself thereby exhibits the virtue of being "ungrabby." But notice that the policy of keeping one's hands to oneself establishes a standard of conduct for *those on the playground*; more importantly, it is in virtue of its *collective application* that individuals are bound to comply with its requirements. Consequently, when Adam violates the norm by grabbing Billy, and Billy retaliates, it would be absurd to criticize Billy for failing to keep his hands to himself. With Adam's violation, the collective norm is suspended, and in extricating himself, Billy does not himself *break* the rule. Indeed, Billy might nonetheless embody the virtue of being ungrabby; his action against Adam does not show otherwise.

To better capture this, notice that the norm, "keep your hands to yourself" is an abbreviated version of the more complex norm, "keep your hands to yourself on the condition that others are keeping their hands to themselves." We see, then, that the moral virtue of being "ungrabby" is *reciprocal*; it identifies a standard of conduct that applies to groups, and individuals are required to abide by the norm it specifies, as long as others generally do so as well.

Notice that, in this playground case, the virtue does not indicate what one is permitted to do in response to its violation. Surely there are certain retaliatory acts that Billy could perform against Adam that would be inappropriate or even impermissible. That Adam's violation suspends the collective norm does not afford to Billy moral *carte blanche* to respond however he wishes. Though his retaliatory response does not itself constitute a violation of the "keep your hands to yourself" norm, Billy may still retaliate in ways that render him worthy of criticism, perhaps even punishment. So Adam's grabbiness may warrant Billy giving him a good push to get him off, but it doesn't warrant a crushing blow to the head. That's clear, but given that there are many other acts between these two extreme poles, it requires judgment and some context to determine where the line is between the acceptable and unacceptable.

Return now to political disagreement among democratic citizens. We have said previously that in order to remain *democratic,* these engagements must exhibit a fundamental recognition of and respect for the political equality of all citizens. In order to exhibit this respect, disagreements must be governed by certain rules. Citizens who manifest the stable disposition to satisfy the relevant norms thereby exhibit public virtue. Now, clearly, some public virtues are first-personal. For example, one's engagements with other citizens must manifest the public virtue of honesty. That one's fellow citizens are inveterate dissemblers does not license one to lie. In fact, where dishonesty is rampant in public life, speaking the truth becomes all the more important.

Contrast the public virtue of honesty with that of fairness. To get a better fix on the contrast we have in mind, imagine that you're playing a game of checkers with someone who routinely and systematically cheats. You dutifully play by the rules, but she just keeps on breaking them, always to her own advantage. Are you still required to play by the rules? Perhaps in some cases, it would be a mark of your *integrity* or *sportsmanship* to continue playing fairly. But when the other person's rule-breaking is constant and extreme, there is a sense in which the two of you are simply not *playing a game* at all – or at least you're not playing the *same* game. What then could bind you to the rules of checkers? It would seem that in this case, all bets are off – it's a board game free-for-all, and perhaps there simply are *no rules* governing the activity. Of course, just as in the playground case, this does not entail that one is licensed to do *anything*; it simply means that the rules of checkers are no longer in effect. Hence it would certainly be *permissible* for you to at least alter your conduct to reflect the norms by which your opponent seems to be playing.

That's an admittedly simplistic example. However, we think it easily generalizes. Fairness is a reciprocal public virtue. Reciprocal public virtues prescribe modes of conduct to us, *collectively*, in our role as citizens. Accordingly, individuals are required to exhibit these virtues only when they are embraced and generally practiced by the society at large. Where the norm corresponding to a reciprocal public virtue is generally violated within a group, the virtue itself is rendered inactive, as it establishes a standard of behavior *only under the conditions where the norm is collectively embraced.*

The Debasement Puzzle

We are now in a position to better understand the debasement puzzle. Let's begin by recalling that argumentation is a collective enterprise. When it occurs in response to political disagreement among democratic citizens, it must evince the participants' respect for one another's standing as political equals. We might say, then, that civil political disagreement is itself an inherently *reciprocal* endeavor. We attempt to rationally work through our political disputes, with all their attendant passion and vigor, in a way that nonetheless expresses our respect for the equality of our interlocutor. We can simplify this point by saying that *civility* in political disagreement is a reciprocal public virtue. It specifies a standard of conduct in argument that is predicated on the assumption that interlocutors in general will embrace it. No citizen is required to manifest the public virtue of civility within a community that generally disregards it. And this is especially so when those who are wielding the institutional power of the government routinely flout the virtue of civility.

Thus the puzzle finds its solution. We all value civility, but we also regard our political opposition as either unwilling or incapable of abiding by its requirements. Once we are convinced that our opponents will not reciprocate civility in argument, we no longer have a rationale for upholding the standards that civility sets, even though we nonetheless value the virtue. Our opponents, of course, reason similarly. The result is the truly tragic political condition of widespread political incivility. However, the tragedy is compounded by the fact that much of the incivility is blameless: ordinary citizens often have adequate reason to assume that their opposition has pulled back from the commitment to civility, and so they also have adequate reason to hold that the requirements of civility are no longer in play in public life.

The Path to Debasement

The final point of the preceding section was intentionally provocative. It requires some unpacking. We live in a political environment where citizens tend to get their information about their political rivals from news and other media sources. Unfortunately, those sources are increasingly allied with the political leanings of their audiences, so conservatives, liberals, alt-righters, radical leftists, social democrats, social justice warriors, socialists, and even moderates now have their very own news sites. Driven by commercial interests and the resulting need to deliver to advertisers a definable demographic of viewers, these sources strive to keep the attention of their respective target audiences. And nothing succeeds quite like providing a steady feed of disparaging images of the target demographic's political opposition. Accordingly, our political discourse is saturated with the *ad hominem*, the fallacy of attacking the person.

Although the *ad hominem* is among the most commonly cited fallacies in popular discussion, it is not nearly so widely understood. Yet clarity about the *ad hominem* is helpful in thinking about how we might emerge from our current political condition.

So let's begin at the beginning. Fallacies are improper inferences, popular ways of drawing conclusions from premises that in fact offer them no support. In its most common variety, the *ad hominem* fallacy takes the following form:

Premise: Person S is in some specified way vicious.
Conclusion: We should reject the things S says.

The vices identified in the premise of course vary. Depending on the context, it might be claimed that S is a hypocrite, an alcoholic, a person with a "low IQ," a racist, a pervert, a neoliberal, a lowbrow, a neocon, a snob, a pinhead, and so on. To be sure, some of these traits may not be actual vices, but the effective deployment of the *ad hominem* depends only on the speaker's audience believing that the trait attributed in the premise is indeed vicious. The *ad hominem*'s strategy is that of identifying the purported vice ascribed to S in the premise as sufficient grounds for rejecting the things S has said.

The prevalence of the *ad hominem* in political debate is easy to explain. Given the carefully curated and time-constrained forums in which most public political discourse occurs, it is just easier for disputants to talk about each other than about the ideas and policies over which they disagree. Consequently, discussions of politics all too regularly become clashes over personalities. Yet, despite its understandable prevalence, the garden-variety *ad hominem* is obviously fallacious.

What makes the *ad hominem* fallacious is that there is no stable connection between a vicious personality trait and the quality of view. Consider the alcoholism smear. Someone may say: Sam doesn't know enough about politics to be trusted – just look at how much she drinks! But there's nothing about being an alcoholic that precludes Sam from knowing a great deal about politics. (In fact, it might be that Sam drinks so much because she knows so much about politics!) A purported vice needn't entail that the speaker is unreliable in the domain in question. And so, *ad hominem* arguments are fallacious in virtue of the fact that the vice ascribed in the premise is irrelevant to the conclusion about what the person has said. In professional treatments of these matters, the *ad hominem* is characterized as a fallacy of *relevance*.

But there's an additional respect in which the *ad hominem* is an instance of bad reasoning. It is often deployed as a strategy for making disagreement emotionally taxing on the person with whom one is arguing. That is, when one deploys an *ad hominem*, one imposes an additional burden on one's interlocutor. For now, not only must she defend her view against your criticism, she must also bear the pressure of having her person subjected to scrutiny. For many, this makes debate too unpleasant, and so they learn to avoid critical exchange altogether. This has the consequence of granting the floor entirely to the verbal bullies. Insofar as argument and debate aim at goals like getting the truth, deepening understanding, and gaining a better grasp of the reasons and evidence relevant to an issue at hand, the impact of the *ad hominem* is decidedly antirational.

Under present conditions, the *ad hominem* is commonly used to perform an additional troubling function. Consider that *ad hominem* attacks are most frequently deployed for the sake of an audience of sympathetic onlookers. When a liberal calls his conservative interlocutor a "wing-nut," it's not for the sake of winning over the conservatives; rather, the smear is meant to serve as a cue to the liberals who might be observing the exchange. To be more precise, the *ad hominem* serves to convince one's allies that one's interlocutor is vicious and unsavory, and therefore either uninterested in or incapable of civility. It is worth noting that many of the most popular modes of *ad hominem* in currency attack the opposition's *intelligence* and *patriotism*. This has the effect of encouraging among those for whom the *ad hominem* is effective the view that the opposition *cannot be reasoned with* and thus cannot practice civility as a reciprocal public virtue.

The Need for an Argumentative Culture

The upshot of this chapter is that in order to satisfy the full range of our civic duties as democratic citizens, we need others generally to do the same. And when it comes to civil political disagreement, we can practice the corresponding virtues only within a broader social environment that is conducive to proper argumentation. In short, in order to disagree civilly, we need to argue well; and in order to argue well, we must be able to count on others to do their part too. But this takes a kind of mutual trust in one another's capacity and willingness to engage civilly. So in order to avoid debasement, we must be able to see each other as operating within a well-ordered *argumentative culture*.

10

Repairing Argumentative Culture

We have traveled a long way quickly. Here's where things stand. Democracy is the thesis that a decent and stable political order is possible among equal citizens who nonetheless disagree, often sharply, about the precise shape their shared social life should take. As we have emphasized several times, this places political disagreement at the heart of democracy. Yet, as this disagreement is always among political *equals*, citizens are required to conduct their political arguments in ways that reflect the equality of their opponents. We have used the term *civility* to refer to the methods and attitudes that political argumentation must manifest if it is to embody an appropriate recognition of the interlocutors' political equality. Thus far, this book has been aimed at identifying some ways in which political disagreement fails to be civil, and the corresponding ways in which participants in political argument fail at civility. The broad upshot of these discussions is that political disagreement among citizens can be civil only amidst a general culture that promotes proper argumentation. Insofar as our political environment is awash in argument simulations, the project of democratic citizenship is jeopardized. But what can be done?

Some Rudiments of Deductive Logic

Let's start with a quick overview of some rudimentary formal logic. In order to disagree civilly, we must argue well. Arguing well requires that we develop the skills needed to evaluate arguments, both our own and those offered by others. Now, when evaluating an argument, one of the central questions to ask is whether the stated premises indeed support the proposed conclusion. When the premises fail to provide the right kind of support for the conclusion, we often call the argument (and its form) *fallacious*. Fallacies are so pervasive precisely because they are cases in which it *looks* as if the stated premises provide adequate support for a proposed conclusion, but in fact they don't. Take, for example, a simple textbook fallacy, that of *asserting the consequent*:

If Bill's a bachelor, Bill is male.
Bill is male, therefore Bill is a bachelor.

The trouble with an argument of this form is that it presents what's called a *formally invalid inference* – the premises, if true, don't guarantee the truth of the conclusion (since Bill could be a married man). So even were the premises and the conclusion true, the proposed argument fails. Note that the failure is a matter of the proposed argument's *form* rather than its *content* (that's why we characterize the fallacy as *formal*). Accordingly, *any* proposed argument that takes the form "If A, then B; B, therefore A" is an instance of the formal fallacy of asserting the consequent. It doesn't matter what one puts in the place of the variables. Now, the objective of detecting formal fallacies is to reveal cases in which the truth of the stated premises fails to provide the proper kind of support for the conclusion.

We also can identify different degrees in which premises provide support for a conclusion. The highest degree of support that premises can provide for a conclusion is the *guarantee of its truth*, given the truth of the premises. Arguments that manifest that feature are called *deductively valid*. But note that deductive validity does not depend on the stated premises *actually being true*. That is, with a valid argument, the conclusion is guaranteed to be true, *if the premises are true*. Accordingly, an argument can be deductively valid even if every one of its stated premises is false. Here's an example:

All Tories are lizards.
Marlon Brando is Tory.
So, Marlon Brando is a lizard.

The key is to see that even though the premises of this reasoning are false, even though we are aware that some may debate the first premise, *the form* the reasoning takes is perfectly fine. That is, *if the premises were true*, the conclusion would be guaranteed to be true. The key is that with argument-evaluation, we look at two things separately: (1) whether the premises are true, and (2) whether the reasoning takes the right valid form. Some arguments can fail one but have success at the other. So some arguments can have true premises, but bad form; and other arguments can have false premises but good form. The key is to find arguments that succeed at both – true premises and valid form. Now, that's something!

Thus we require an additional metric of formal success. It would seem that an argument that is both deductively valid *and* has premises that in fact are all true would be bombproof. Such arguments are called *deductively sound*. Consider the following deductively sound inference:

Vanderbilt University is located in Nashville, Tennessee.

Nashville, Tennessee is a city in the US.

Therefore, there is at least one university in the US.

Notice that deductive soundness encompasses deductive validity in that every sound argument is also valid. As a matter of definition, a deductively sound argument is a deductively valid argument that has true premises. Since a deductively valid argument is one that guarantees the truth of its conclusion *provided that* its premises are in fact true, it should be no surprise that deductive soundness is often considered the gold standard for argumentative success. Every deductively sound argument actually *establishes* the truth of its conclusion. Who could ask for more than that?

One thing to understand is that, with the introduction of all this high-falutin' logical vocabulary, we're trying to articulate a set of *ideals*, again. Ideals of deductive validity and argumentative soundness. Those are high-ideals, and what's necessary, again, is that we have to understand the ideals in order to understand all the ways we are to be evaluated in light of them.

The Turn to Informal Logic

There are problems with taking deductive soundness as the benchmark of argument quality. Recall, an argument is *sound* when it (a) has *true premises* and (b) has a form that, if its premises are true, its conclusion is *guaranteed to be true*. For one thing, we don't regularly have access to the kinds of high-quality premises that deductive soundness demands. There are no guarantees in life, and the world's a messy place; we're often stuck with rough-and-ready pieces of reasoning that are just *good enough* for our given purposes. Sometimes good reasoning isn't about giving a perfect guarantee, but one that is just one that is very probable. When we rely on our past experience to reason that taking an aspirin is a good way to relieve a headache, we are typically depending on what amounts to pretty sparse evidence rather than well-founded data. We take the aspirin for the headache, even though we don't have a perfect *guarantee* that the aspirin will do the trick. But it seems perfectly reasonable to do so. We don't want to make the perfect the enemy of the good, so we must look for more forgiving standards of argumentative success. And so we look to the fallible, but reliable, inductive arguments – arguments where true premises yield conclusions that are *more likely true than false*.

But there is another problem. As it turns out, deductive soundness isn't all that it's cracked up to be. Not even deductive soundness guarantees that an argument does what it needs to do. To see this, imagine a dispute over the question of who was the only President of the United States to serve two nonconsecutive terms. One disputant says: *Chester A. Arthur*. Another says: *Grover Cleveland*. An argument is needed to resolve the dispute. Now imagine our second disputant making the following argument:

Grover Cleveland was the only President of the United States to serve nonconsecutive terms. Therefore, Grover Cleveland was the only President of the United States to serve nonconsecutive terms.

That's obviously a flawed, impotent argument. But notice that it's got one thing going for it: it's deductively sound! The truth of its premise indeed guarantees the truth of its conclusion. And, moreover, the premise is in fact true. (Look it up, folks.) Yet, again, the argument is patently lacking. It looks as if the supposed gold standard for argumentative success just failed.

This means that there must be more to argumentative success than meeting the requirements of deductive soundness. And looking to the function of argument provides a clue to what else is needed. When arguing, we are looking to address questions, resolve disagreements, further inquiry, and flesh things out. The trouble with the Grover Cleveland argument above is that it *begs the question*. The conclusion is identical to the premise, so the argument attempts to resolve a disputed question by merely asserting one disputant's answer. But disputes arise between people who disagree, and arguments must be designed to address disputes in ways that could provide a *resolution* to disagreements. In order to resolve a disagreement, the arguments provided must actually address the disputants and attempt to provide them with reasons to come to agree. Accordingly, even a formally unimpeachable argument can fail if it is unable to fulfill the social role of argumentation. To put the matter in a nutshell: in order to be successful, arguments must be sufficiently *dialectical*.

What is it for an argument to be sufficiently dialectical? Here are two rough desiderata. First, an argument must be composed not merely of reasons that support its conclusion, but of reasons that its target audience can *recognize* as reasons. Accordingly, a flat-footed appeal to the authority of the Pope in a dispute among Catholics and non-Catholics about the permissibility of stem-cell research is a dialectical failure. Second, an argument must address the most pressing concerns and doubts that prevail among the target audience. That is, in order to attempt to resolve a disagreement, we must not only assess the reasons for the side we endorse, we must also assess the reasons for both sides. So a dialectically proper argument presents not merely a case for one's preferred view; it also takes into account the going objections to one's conclusion. Arguments that fail to satisfy these desiderata *beg the question* and thus fail to be dialectical.

Thus we can see that this dialectical requirement for success in argument brings with it additional responsibilities for arguers. In order to argue well, one must be in a good position to know or have compelling reasons to believe that one's conclusion is true. But in order to properly assess one's own reasons, one also must know something about those with whom one disagrees. More specifically, one needs to know something about their reasons, and why they might (reasonably, perhaps) reject what to you seems so clearly true. Ideally, one must be able to access a *plausible* rationale, even if not ultimately *convincing*, for the positions that oppose one's own. We can take this one step further by saying that, in order to properly evaluate one's own position, one needs to confront a well-formulated version of the opposing view. In the absence of a well-crafted foil, our own reasoning is likely to become distorted.

Given these admittedly basic points, we already can see that successful political argument isn't what many people say it is. Frequently, political argumentation is engaged for the sake of "owning" the other side, shutting down the opposition, and closing the discussion. But if the aim of argumentation is actually to ensure that one's position indeed tracks the best reasons and evidence, success simply cannot lie in silencing one's opposition or proving them silly or foolish. Prevailing in an argument, rather, requires something in the order of coming to see, and perhaps even appreciate, the opposition's rationale. That, of course, is just the beginning to a well-run argument. But notice that this means that successful argument does not put an end to discussion, but rather helps to continue one.

Pathologizing the Opposition

What has been said thus far goes to show how far we are from having a minimally acceptable argumentative culture, let alone a healthy one. It also helps us to identify a crucial respect in which we are falling short. As the previous chapters have demonstrated, so much of what passes for political argumentation today is mainly directed at *evading* the kind of mutual understanding necessary for civil political disagreement by saturating our political discourse with mere *simulations* of argument. When the simulations are taken as the real thing, citizens come to see those with whom they disagree as *incapable* of civil disagreement, and so not worth engaging. What is important to notice now is that these evasion strategies have something in common: they *pathologize* political opposition. That is, the argument simulations try to convince us to not engage with those who disagree by presenting political disagreement itself as the product of the opponents' being in some way *sick*. Diagnosing an opponent's argument is one thing, and proper argumentation calls for it; but it's quite another thing to regard the *opponent* as needing a diagnosis, a clinical explanation for why she holds her views rather than ours. If we seek to repair our culture of political argument, we need to ween ourselves away from the tendency to regard our political opponents as things to be *diagnosed* rather than argued with.

The pervasiveness of this tendency to pathologize political opponents can be gleaned simply by noting the frequency with which terms proposing actual diagnoses are used in political disputes. Right now, both the left and the right are prone to characterize one another with terms loosely drawn from the *Diagnostical and Statistical Manual of Mental Disorders* (DSM): paranoia, narcissism, disassociation, derangement, and so on. These diagnostic tropes serve to impugn the intelligence and rationality of one's opposition. And there's little point in arguing with someone who is irrational or hopelessly inept. However, the tendency to pathologize opponents in these ways often runs deeper in that the *cognitive* assessment of incompetence is typically coupled with an evaluation of the opponent as somehow also *infected* and thus *infectious*. That is, the pathologizing tropes not only serve to portray opponents as people with whom one cannot profitably argue; they also tend to depict opponents as people with whom to *avoid contact* altogether.

To get a sense of how this works, consider the red hats worn by supporters of Donald Trump. These unassuming hats simply have the Trump campaign slogan, "Make America Great Again" ("MAGA" for short) printed in white on the front. One of us (Aikin) owns one of these hats. It was given to him as a well-meaning gift by a friendly family member; so now he owns a MAGA hat. Ironically enough, it fits quite well, and on the day it was given to him, it was quite sunny. So Aikin has worn the hat. Here's the important part: when putting the MAGA hat on, and all the time he was wearing it, he felt as though he was doing something dirty. And he wanted to make sure nobody saw him in the hat. But why? It's just a red hat! Yes, it's just a red hat, but as a symbol it is powerful.

Drawing on this experience, we (Aikin and Talisse) have developed an exercise we regularly do with our academic friends. We ask them to put on, or just hold, the MAGA hat. We've done it at a few academic conferences, and given how reliably left-leaning academics are, we get very few takers. A couple of people have grudgingly put the hat on, a few have held it. But nobody seems very happy about it. In even *handling* the hat, most act as if they are going through some ordeal. One of our colleagues poured hand sanitizer all over her hands after holding it; another threatened us with violence if we asked him to hold it again. These were all in jest (we suppose!), but they express a kind of revulsion even at the symbol of the current President of the United States. They behave as though they have been polluted, made dirty, or infected just by touching the hat.

On one occasion, while giving a lecture on the very topic of this chapter, we asked a relatively renowned academic friend of ours to put the hat on, and he gamely did so. But then somebody else whipped out a phone and snapped a picture of him! Things instantly got real. You can anticipate why. Putting the hat on for this exercise is one thing, but he saw the possibility of a photo of him in a MAGA hat going public, without context, as deeply problematic, even professionally dangerous. We had to have a pretty involved discussion with the person who took the photo, insisting they delete it. It was that serious.

But what's the big deal? It's just a hat. The answer is that political symbols matter, especially in a climate where political opponents regard one another as not merely *wrong*, but *infected*. When we see our opponents as *contagious*, with something that contaminates rationality, we can hardly be expected to engage with them civilly. The sad fact, of course, is that once we regard others in this way, we invite belief polarization, and this phenomenon actually does dismantle our rationality by causing us to hold more extreme commitments than our evidence warrants.

Hearing the Other Side

OK. Back to the initial question. What can be done to repair our argumentative culture? In order to restore our capacity to disagree civilly with our political opponents, we need first to restore our sense that there are still political arguments to be had. This means we must give up the idea that all the defensible, reasonable, right-minded political views come from our own side of the political spectrum. This of course is consistent with sustaining *real commitment* to our political views. What must be jettisoned is the fantasy that the political questions we face admit of only *one* proper response that is so *obvious* that only the depraved or utterly incompetent would fail to see it. The real world of politics simply isn't like that. Those matters worth arguing over are typically so complicated and multifaceted that one should expect there to be *several* plausible views available to reasonable and sincere people who are thinking sincerely.

This may seem to be so simple a conceptual point as to be not worth stating. But again, notice the degree to which our current modes of political discourse are aimed at *denying* the obvious idea that when it comes to important questions of politics, we should expect sincere and intelligent people to disagree. It turns out that although it may strike us as a mere truism when stated on paper, we must *work* to keep ourselves mindful of the fact that political disagreement is possible among reasonable citizens.

Try this. Think of your most confident belief concerning a matter that's currently in dispute among your fellow citizens, the commitment that appears to you to be the most *obviously* correct. But instead of enumerating all the reasons there are to hold that belief, try to think of the best reasons *against* it. Note: the task is not to think of what the loudest or most common critics in fact offer as criticisms of your position. Think, instead, of what you honestly regard as the *best* or *strongest* consideration that counts against your view. Got it? Now, what's your response to it? Here's the important part: if you're able only to think of objections to your view that admit of *easy* replies, you're not really doing your job as a democratic citizen. As democratic citizens, our assumption in thinking through the political questions that confront us should be that even the best views are subject to cogent pushback. If you hold a political belief for which you can anticipate no criticism that's truly forceful, you've not done your due diligence. You're likely caught in an argument simulation.

One way to prevent this is to sincerely seek out good, or at least plausible, arguments from one's opposition. Again, to see one's opponent as rational is different from seeing him as correct; so sincerely looking for cogent reasons from the other side doesn't require one to abandon or dilute one's convictions. It's possible to assess the opposition's reasons as *reasons* and yet hold that the opponent is flatly mistaken. But in pursuing this, we must also acknowledge that finding the good reasons the opposition has to offer will require us to actually *listen to the opponents themselves*. We must recognize that we are not the best judges of what reasons there are on the other side of an issue that we care about. And we should *especially* avoid getting our sense of the reasons on the other side from those on our own side who are all too eager to condemn the opposition. In short, weening ourselves off of the tendency to pathologize our opponents, we will need to actually talk to them.

No doubt a little humility will be helpful here. In looking for the best reasons our opposition has to offer, we will need to do a lot to *invite* their best thoughts, and this will require us to adopt the attitude that we have something yet to learn from our opponents. This kind of humility can be motivated by reflection on the ways our own views have changed and developed over time. We have all had the experience of learning better how to articulate our own ideas, and sometimes we may have even changed our minds about an important issue. What moved us? In all such cases, we learned something new. How did that happen? We had a good conversation with someone where a crucial fact was well communicated, or we struggled to respond to one of their criticisms. None of us ever learned anything by shouting down and demeaning others or by convincing ourselves that our own view is so obviously correct that only those suffering from a pathology would reject it.

Although repairing our argumentative culture requires a group effort, the endeavor begins at home. We can contribute to the repair only by first recognizing *our own vulnerability* to the argumentative pathologies we have identified in this book. And this recognition means that we must come to see some of our own political commitments as the products of those pathologies. In short, we begin to contribute to the repair of our argumentative culture by taking the diagnostic tools that we initially acquired for the purpose of negatively assessing our opposition and turning them inward. Perhaps it sounds odd to say so, but the repair of our argumentative culture starts with self-criticism.

11

Democracy at Dusk

The message of this book is one of cautious optimism. Despite the fact that we think that democracy can't be saved and that the problem is intrinsic to the political arrangement that is democracy, we are still optimists. That's weird, right? Here's how it works. Democracy runs on civil disagreement, and although civil disagreement is difficult, it's not impossibly demanding or otherwise out of reach for democratic citizens. One thing working in favor of civility is that its fundamental value commitments to collective reasoning, open discussion, and earnest argumentation are already widely shared. As we have emphasized throughout these pages, the trouble lies in the fact that it's all too easy to *simulate* civil disagreement, to provide occasions where one can readily take oneself to be engaging in proper argument while really only knocking down straw men and preaching to the choir. Again, what is intriguing about the phenomenon of simulated argument is that it is parasitic on the norms of civil disagreement. Were it not for the fact that citizens generally prize proper argumentation, there would be no need to mimic it. We might say, then, that the trouble with prevailing modes of public discourse arises from our commitment to civil disagreement itself. Civility breeds its own discontent.

We have offered in the preceding chapters a series of diagnoses of civility's discontents. These are the vulnerabilities and pathologies that emerge from sincere attempts to argue well about politics. We have also proposed a strategy for repairing our practices of political argumentation, one that acknowledges that, although civil political disagreement requires a collective effort, the task begins with the individual recognition of our own vulnerabilities to argumentation's mimics. Turning the diagnostic tools one has acquired for assessing others' performance in argument on oneself is perhaps psychologically difficult, but it's not impossible. And, after all, if we care about forming the best possible political views, we have to be willing also to criticize ourselves.

So our approach is generally hopeful. However, obstacles to civil political disagreement still loom. Throughout this book we have been developing an analysis of a persistent, but we think underappreciated, problem that confronts democracy. Our analysis has proceeded in a relatively piecemeal way. We have looked at specific sites where our commitment to proper political argumentation is turned against itself. In Chapter 1, we called this the *Owl of Minerva Problem*. This problem is more formidable than it may appear. Although it shows up in our particular attempts to engage in civil political disagreement, it is actually far more *general* a problem, one that cannot be met simply by diagnosing common argumentative pathologies. Indeed, once it is presented in its full light, we are not sure what to recommend in response to it. But surely a first step in addressing a problem is to identify it *as* a problem. Unsurprisingly, then, this book closes with a new challenge, what might be posed as the *Scaled-Up* Owl of Minerva Problem.

Scaling Up the Problem

"The Owl of Minerva flies only at dusk." That's a poetic way of saying that wisdom emerges only in hindsight, that understanding is always backward-looking. We develop explanatory vocabularies in order to address what has already transpired, to illuminate what has surprised or affronted us. But once we have deployed those vocabularies and formulated the requisite explanations, whole new problems come into view that call for additional conceptual tools that have yet to be developed. Put simply, the achievement of understanding is often *itself* the occasion for the emergence of further difficulties, difficulties that would not have emerged but for our prior explanatory success.

As we have emphasized throughout this book, argumentation arises organically. As we are reasoning creatures, disagreement emerges as a matter of course, and when we find ourselves disagreeing over things that matter, we are driven to attempt to resolve the dispute. In pursuing resolutions to our disagreements, we need not only to think hard about the matters in dispute; we must also think about the mechanics of disagreements themselves. We must ask: what makes for adequate evidence? What makes an argument compelling? What makes criticism fair? Which sources of information are reliable? And so on. However, once we've begun to study these latter phenomena and communicate our findings, we actually change the domain of our disagreement. Our conception of the mechanics of argumentation becomes another matter over which others can disagree. Accordingly, disagreements about, say, the proper response to global poverty becomes two-tiered; once you have made explicit the *evidence* upon which your view about global poverty is based, an interlocutor can dispute the *relevance* of that evidence, its *weight*, and even its status as *evidence*. Importantly, these "second-order" disagreements over the nature of evidence need not indicate a disagreement over the "first-order" issue of global poverty. People who agree about the proper response to global poverty might nonetheless disagree sharply about what evidence there is, and even about what counts as evidence. Yet it must be noted that first-order political disagreements are frequently accompanied by second-order disagreements over what evidence there is, what the relevant considerations are, which purported sources of information are reliable, and so on. For example, insofar as there are disagreements over climate policy, there are disputes over these second-order questions.

In this book, we have proposed new conceptual tools for evaluating political disagreements. Among these tools are the "polarization dynamic" and the concept of argument *simulations*, including the weak man and burning man fallacies. We discussed these in Chapter 6. But they are all of a type – because in these instances, we aren't just reasoning about the things we disagree about; we reason about our disagreement, we reason about how we've reasoned. That's a pretty significant shift of focus, and that requires a different kind of vocabulary. To use a term from academic philosophy, we have introduced a *metalanguage* for talking about our disagreements. As we saw in Chapter 7, metalanguages are vocabularies for talking about the ways we talk. Like the concepts concerning evidence discussed above, they are second-order. That is, one can assess an argument as fallacious without thereby rejecting its conclusion or its premises, and one can assess an argument as cogent or reasonable while still rejecting its conclusion. As we noted earlier, this distinction allows us to evaluate arguments along two separate lines – one whether we accept the premises and the conclusion, another whether the reasoning is good. Those are separate questions. So, the metalanguage about argumentation enables us to distinguish between the two levels of evaluation discussed at the beginning of this book between the truth of an argument's conclusion and the quality of the reasoning offered in its support. And it is by means of this very distinction that one can assess an interlocutor as mistaken in her conclusion and yet sincere, responsible, and competent in her reasoning. Developing a robust metalanguage for talking about the structure of our disagreements is, for this reason, crucial for sustaining the civility that is necessary for proper democracy. In fact, the very notion of argumentative civility is one that isn't thinkable without a metalanguage.

But here is where the *Scaled-Up Owl of Minerva Problem* gets off the ground. With the development of the new metalanguage, we acquire new explanatory tools for evaluating disagreements, but we also introduce *new sites for disagreement*. As in the global poverty example above, once one gains sufficient mastery of the vocabulary of the various fallacies and other pitfalls that have been discussed in this book, one has a *new* way of tarring one's political opponents. Rather than engaging with their arguments and reasons, one can simply assess them as being caught in the polarization dynamic, or fixated on a burning man. Maybe you've met some people who, once they know the names of the fallacies, just use them as means for arguing for their own view and tearing down others. The tools of logic become weapons, not tools for improving critical discussion. The metalanguage is put to work at the first-order, as a new way of simply marking that there is a disagreement, while expressing distrust or contempt for our interlocutors. The distinction between assessing someone as being *wrong* and assessing them as *depraved* and *incompetent* is thereby dissolved, and thus civility is undermined. A new mode of argument simulation is born, and we are again one step behind.

The Fallacy Fallacy

The *fallacy fallacy* is a good lens through which to observe how the Owl of Minerva Problem scales up. The fallacy fallacy occurs when one starts seeing fallacies everywhere. In the same way that the college sophomore taking Abnormal Psychology becomes convinced that everyone in their dorm suffers from some disassociative disorder, students of informal logic frequently become convinced that fallacies are everywhere. That's fine, in a way. There *are* lots of fallacies and instances of bad reasoning. But once one starts seeing fallacies everywhere, one is tempted to think that those who commit the fallacies are *thereby wrong about the things they say*. But that inference is itself a fallacy! Here's the scheme of the argument:

S believes that p

S gives argument A in support of p

A is fallacious

Therefore, p is false

It's clear that the conclusion does not follow from the premises. Just because someone has terrible reasons for holding a conclusion, it doesn't mean that the conclusion is false. Your uncle may believe something on the basis of wishful thinking, but that doesn't make it a false belief. So if he believes that Manchester United won the 2007–8 UEFA Champions League simply on the basis of the fact that the Red Devils are his favorite team, his reasoning is flawed, but his conclusion is nonetheless correct.

To repeat, that's the whole point of evaluating arguments *as arguments*, not just as *mere claims*. We must keep our assessment of the reasons separate from our assessment of the conclusion. More generally, we must not lose sight of the fact that the fallaciousness of a piece of reasoning is consistent with the truth of its conclusion and the truth of its premises. But that's precisely where the fallacy fallacy goes wrong. It deploys a second-order assessment of reasons in impugning a first-order conclusion. Accordingly, it also erodes the crucial distinction between being mistaken and being incompetent.

There's a further point that's worth making here. The fallacy fallacy provides a case where training in logic actually *creates a new kind of logical error*. Nobody could commit the fallacy fallacy if there were no vocabulary of fallacies to begin with. The metalanguage of logic, which generally helps to make us *better reasoners*, also makes possible a particular kind of argumentative pathology. The very project of detecting and correcting fallacious reasoning provides the occasion for the emergence of a brand new fallacy. Ironic, wouldn't you say?

Recall that the whole point of developing a metalanguage about disagreement is to enable us to monitor and thus improve our first-order disputes. But no matter how carefully we may craft them, metalanguages are tools to be employed by us fallible, hasty, and easily distracted creatures. And so, although the metalanguage of disagreement may help us to argue well, we have seen that it also brings its own distinctive problems, some of which can be understood and corrected only in hindsight. After all, it is only *after* the idea of a fallacy has emerged and taken hold in our general argumentative idiom that one can commit the fallacy fallacy.

More on Fake News

To see another manifestation of the Scaled-Up Owl of Minerva Problem, let's return to the topic of fake news. Recall from our discussion in Chapter 7 that, despite the popular consensus that fake news is a significant problem for democracy, there is no shared definition of what fake news is. We sketched our own "institutional" conception of fake news, but we recognize that any proposed definition is beset with difficulties. In fact, it might be the case that the consensus over the danger of fake news is what impedes the establishment of a common definition. The Owl of Minerva Problem helps to explain why.

To begin, let's explore an analogy between the task of defining fake news and that of defining garden-variety lying. We all condemn lying, and we wield the concept with great facility. Yet it is surprisingly difficult to produce a satisfactory definition of lying. Take the popular view that lying is *intentionally asserting what's untrue*. This analysis at first seems obviously correct. But it fails. One could lie while asserting what is true. To wit, let's say that I believe that your wife is at the bar, but in fact she is at the library. You ask me her whereabouts, and I report that she is at the library (a report which I believe is false). I have lied to you, even though I asserted a true proposition. That's because I thought it was false – that's why I asserted it! So lying isn't a matter of asserting what's untrue after all.

Perhaps the initial definition of lying could be rescued with this minor tweak: lying is *intentionally asserting something as* true *that one believes is* false. Although this improves on its predecessor, it also fails. There are contexts where one lies even when asserting a truth that one believes. Think of cases where one makes an assertion that one realizes one's audience will misunderstand. Bill Clinton famously asserted "there *is* no sexual relationship" with Monica Lewinsky, knowing that his audience would understand him to be claiming that *there never was* a relationship. Clinton uttered a true proposition that he also believed, but he nonetheless lied.

Given such considerations, one might distinguish *asserting what is untrue* from *making an assertion designed to mislead*. But there are problems to be confronted there as well, as there are contexts in which one lies without asserting *anything*. We needn't pursue this matter further. Our point has been only that popular definitions of lying fail to capture certain clear instances of lying. When dealing with complex phenomena, simple definitions will not do; complex phenomena call for complex definitions. However, we set about constructing the complex definitions in part by testing our existing definitions against cases where we think the phenomenon to be defined is obviously in play. That's how we just proceeded in the discussion of lying: we took an intuitive definition, and then proposed examples of lying that the definition cannot recognize as such. That is, we tested our definition against examples of the phenomenon to be defined. This is admittedly an odd way of proceeding, as it presupposes that we can identify *examples* of a phenomenon independently of knowing its *definition*.

Thus we confront what philosophers call the *problem of the criterion*. Any attempt to produce a good definition must begin from presumed instances of the phenomenon that is to be defined. In many philosophical contexts, the circularity of the paradox "I know it when I see it" is manageable because philosophical debates often proceed against wider background agreements. For example, philosophers who disagree sharply about justice nonetheless agree that antebellum slavery is an exemplary instance of severe injustice. Similarly, metaphysical disputes over the nature of physical objects typically presume that tables and chairs are among such entities.

However, when it comes to defining fake news, we fear that the endeavor is doomed. Recall that we are looking for an analysis of fake news that is properly *second-order*, and therefore *politically impartial*. That is, we require a definition that could identify instances of fake news independently of the political valence of its perpetrator. Obviously, a definition of fake news fails to be second-order if it stipulates that fake news is a tactic used only by conservatives (or liberals, or Republicans, or what have you). Whatever we say fake news is, our definition must render it possible for parties across the political spectrum to be guilty of deploying it.

Therein lies the trouble. As our discussion of lying demonstrated, in order to construct a nuanced definition, we must build upon specific cases that we take to be clear-cut instances of the phenomenon in question. In other words, we craft a definition of lying partly by testing proposed conceptions against cases that we independently assume to be clear instances of lying. We proceeded partly by saying, "Whatever lying is, *this* definitely should count as a lie!" The same goes for an analysis of fake news. Recall our discussion in Chapter 7. There, we tested the merit of an intuitive definition partly by looking to cases that we already regard as instances of fake news. Accordingly, in order to devise a nuanced definition that is also second-order and politically impartial, we must identify cases of fake news that can be presumed to be noncontroversial among otherwise divided citizens. We doubt that there are such cases.

Here's why. Consider that any proposed conception of fake news will include reference to the intentional dissemination of false or misleading political information by institutions posing as news sources. So if we require a politically impartial account that could win broad assent across political divides, we will need to begin from assumptions about specific instances when purported news institutions have engaged in intentional deception. It seems likely to us that our political divisions run so deep that there are no cases that will be generally agreed to be instances of intentional political deception. What's more, there are similarly deep divisions over what makes an institution an authentic news source, and even *what journalism is*. Hence, any definition that begins from the premise that, say, Pizzagate is a paradigmatic case of fake news will likely be dismissed as politically opportunistic. To any such account, one will find American conservatives who will respond, "If *that's* the paradigm of fake news from which your view proceeds – rather than, say, the whitewashing of the Benghazi incident – then your account is rigged against us." Those are recent American cases, but these trends obtain well beyond the US borders. Accusations of the depth of anti-Semitism within the UK Labour Party and the details of Boris Johnson's colonialist views about Myanmar, for example: those are "fake news" or deep truths, depending on your antecedent political associations.

And there's the Owl of Minerva, scaled-up and in full flight. In order for the concept of "fake news" to do its diagnostic and reparative work, we need a conception of the phenomenon that can be properly second-order, rather than just one more way of impugning one's opponents and dismissing their sources of infor- mation. Yet such a formulation must be built upon cases of the phenomenon in question that are noncontroversial across our first- order political divides. That is, we must be able to point to several obvious instances of fake news, and try to discern their common nature. However, there likely are no cases that are obvious and noncontroversial across our first-order political divides. Thus, every proposed nuanced definition of fake news will appear to some as opportunistic, designed to impugn certain regions of the political spectrum and vindicate others. A definition of fake news that serves only to further tar our political opponents is counterproductive. In fact, when our conception of fake news amounts only to this, it cannot serve as a diagnostic that can help repair political discourse; it becomes just another pathology. Accordingly, the term "fake news" is most commonly deployed by partisans as a way to simply dismiss the other side's factual statements.

Trolls, Sock-puppets, and Bots

The Owl of Minerva Problem, in both its local and scaled-up versions, plagues our political disagreements. It is now common for disputants to charge one another with committing various fallacies and other argumentative fouls, simply as a way of expressing their dislike for their opposition's view. To see another instance of this, just look online. To be sure, new communications technologies have created exciting new modes of political discourse; yet these very innovations bring with them new ways in which political argument can be fouled. Consider that *trolling* and *sock-puppetry* are made possible by the structure of our social media platforms. But note also that although these are ostensibly *second-order* pathologies of online argumentation, the terms are now commonly deployed at the first-order simply to impugn one's interlocutors. That is, one calls another a "troll" as a way of disparaging their view and shutting down further discussion with them.

For an even more recent example, it is now common on social media for disputants to charge one another with being a "bot." To be sure, posts and comments that are the products of bots are problematic, and it's good to call out bots for what they are; however, one frequently finds the accusation that a comment is produced by a bot *simply when a discussant makes an assertion that others on the thread think is false*. Perhaps by the time you are reading this book there will be a term for those who falsely and opportunistically call others bots? Then the coining of an additional term for those who improperly deploy *that* criticism can't be far behind. And on it goes.

The Owl in Full View

The Owl of Minerva Problem is now in full view. In a way, it has been the theme underlying this entire book, so it might be helpful as we draw our discussion to a close to formulate it in a highly general way.

In order for democracy to thrive, citizens must be able to disagree civilly, to argue well together about the social and political world they share. But in order to argue well, they must develop together a second-order vocabulary aimed at assessing arguments – a metalanguage about disagreement – that preserves the distinction between assessments of the views in dispute and assessments of the character of the reasons disputants offer in support of their respective positions. However, the metalanguage lends itself to a specific kind of abuse; once the second-order concepts make their way into argumentative practice, they can be deployed at the first-order as just additional ways of dismissing, slighting, and impugning those with whom one disagrees. This occasions a need for additional second-order concepts that can identify these new abuses. But, of course, the minting of further second-order concepts only occasions new abuses.

Thus the Owl of Minerva Problem scales-up. Our conceptual vocabulary for evaluating argumentative performance is doomed to run behind the degenerative argumentative practices. In this sense, our diagnostic tools for civil disagreement will forever operate at dusk, only after the abuses have been committed and the damage done. What's worse, the creating of new diagnostic tools will always create new possibilities for abuse. Our tools for promoting civility are inevitably condemned to produce new forms of incivility, and the pathologies of public discourse are always at least one step ahead of our capacity to understand and correct them. The tragedy is inescapable.

You can see this dynamic at work in the fact that by the time you're reading this page, it's bound to be the case that the dysfunctions we have discussed will have become outdated, perhaps even quaint. New modes of abuse, new simulations of argument, and new tactics for shutting down civil disagreement will have superseded what we have theorized in these pages. As we write this sentence, another protracted national campaigning season is shifting into gear. Anxieties over deepfakes, social media bots, micro-targeted disinformation blitzes, and other technology-fueled disruptions of democracy are justifiably running high. We can only imagine what the coming months will bring.

It's hard not to simply give up and join the ranks of those who hold that the democratic ideal is some kind of sham, a naive cover for the exercise of raw power captured by ruling elites. To be clear, we conceded that democracy as it is currently practiced is a far cry from the ideal of collective self-government among political equals by means of civil disagreement. It's less clear that our failings constitute sufficient reason to jettison the idea altogether. After all, it is only against the backdrop of the ideal that our current political practice can count as *falling short*. That's cold comfort, we realize. However, there's perhaps some further consolation in the thought that the pathologies we have discussed in these pages, including even the Owl of Minerva Problem, are *intelligible* no matter what political orientation our reader might embrace. No matter how people might disagree about first-order political questions, there is nonetheless sufficient basis for a mutual understanding of the joint task of democracy. And perhaps that's the central lesson. The task of democratic citizenship is an ongoing travail. Just as bodily health consists largely in the regular quotidian efforts of cleanliness, nourishment, and exercise, so it goes for the civil health of a democratic community. Nobody would believe you if you said you had invented a pill that will make you healthy no matter what you eat or how infrequently you exercise. Well, so it goes, too, for democracy. It takes work.

Index